GCSE AQA
Chemistry
The Revision Guide

This book is for anyone doing **GCSE AQA Chemistry**.

GCSE Science is all about **understanding how science works**.
And not only that — understanding it well enough to be able to **question**
what you hear on TV and read in the papers.

But you can't do that without a fair chunk of **background knowledge**. Hmm, tricky.

Happily this CGP book includes all the **science facts** you need to learn,
and shows you how they work in the **real world**. And in true CGP style,
we've explained it all as **clearly and concisely** as possible.

It's also got some daft bits in to try and make the whole
experience at least vaguely entertaining for you.

<u>What CGP is all about</u>

Our sole aim here at CGP is to produce the highest
quality books — carefully written, immaculately presented
and dangerously close to being funny.

Then we work our socks off to get them
out to you — at the cheapest possible prices.

Contents

Published by CGP

From original material by Richard Parsons.

Editors:
Ellen Bowness, Katherine Craig, Jane Sawers, Karen Wells.

Contributors:
Mike Bossart, Sandy Gardner, Gemma Hallam.

ISBN: 978 1 84762 615 8

With thanks to Chris Elliss, Katie Braid, Ellen Bowness, Philip Dobson, Mary Falkner, Glenn Rogers and Ian Starkey for the proofreading.
With thanks to Jan Greenway, Laura Jakubowski and Laura Stoney for the copyright research.

Graph to show trend in atmospheric CO_2 concentration and global temperature on page 29 based on data by EPICA Community Members 2004 and Siegenthaler et al 2005.

Groovy website: www.cgpbooks.co.uk

Printed by Elanders Ltd, Newcastle upon Tyne.
Jolly bits of clipart from CorelDRAW®

The Scientific Process

You need to know a few things about how the world of science works. First up is the <u>scientific process</u> — how a scientist's <u>mad idea</u> turns into a <u>widely accepted theory</u>.

Scientists Come Up with <u>Hypotheses</u> — Then <u>Test</u> Them

About 100 years ago, scientists hypothesised that atoms looked like this.

1) Scientists try to <u>explain</u> things. Everything.
2) They start by <u>observing</u> something they don't understand — it could be anything, e.g. planets in the sky, a person suffering from an illness, what matter is made of... anything.
3) Then, they come up with a <u>hypothesis</u> — a <u>possible explanation</u> for what they've observed.
4) The next step is to <u>test</u> whether the hypothesis might be <u>right or not</u> — this involves <u>gathering evidence</u> (i.e. <u>data</u> from <u>investigations</u>).
5) The scientist uses the hypothesis to make a <u>prediction</u> — a statement based on the hypothesis that can be <u>tested</u>. They then <u>carry out an investigation</u>.
6) If data from experiments or studies <u>backs up the prediction</u>, you're one step closer to figuring out if the hypothesis is true.

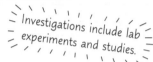

Investigations include lab experiments and studies.

Other Scientists Will <u>Test</u> the Hypothesis Too

1) <u>Other</u> scientists will use the hypothesis to make their <u>own predictions</u>, and carry out their <u>own experiments</u> or studies.
2) They'll also try to <u>reproduce</u> the original investigations to check the results.
3) And if <u>all the experiments</u> in the world back up the hypothesis, then scientists start to think it's <u>true</u>.
4) However, if a scientist somewhere in the world does an experiment that <u>doesn't</u> fit with the hypothesis (and other scientists can <u>reproduce</u> these results), then the hypothesis is in trouble.
5) When this happens, scientists have to come up with a new hypothesis (maybe a <u>modification</u> of the old hypothesis, or maybe a completely <u>new</u> one).

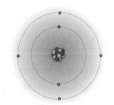

After more evidence was gathered, scientists changed their hypothesis to this.

If <u>Evidence</u> Supports a Hypothesis, It's <u>Accepted</u> — <u>for Now</u>

1) If pretty much every scientist in the world believes a hypothesis to be true because experiments back it up, then it usually goes in the <u>textbooks</u> for students to learn.
2) Accepted hypotheses are often referred to as <u>theories</u>.

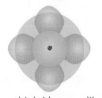

Now we think it's more like this.

3) Our <u>currently accepted</u> theories are the ones that have survived this 'trial by evidence' — they've been tested many, many times over the years and survived (while the less good ones have been ditched).
4) However... they never, <u>never</u> become hard and fast, totally indisputable <u>fact</u>. You can never know... it'd only take <u>one</u> odd, totally inexplicable result, and the hypothesising and testing would start all over again.

<u>You expect me to believe that — then show me the evidence...</u>

If scientists think something is true, they need to produce evidence to convince others — it's all part of <u>testing a hypothesis</u>. One hypothesis might survive these tests, while others won't — it's how things progress. And along the way some hypotheses will be disproved — i.e. shown not to be true.

<u>Your Data's Got To be Good</u>

<u>Evidence</u> is the key to science — but not all evidence is equally good.
The way evidence is <u>gathered</u> can have a big effect on how <u>trustworthy</u> it is...

<u>Lab Experiments</u> **and** *Studies* **Are Better Than** <u>Rumour</u>

See page 5 for more about fair tests and variables.

1) Results from <u>experiments</u> in <u>laboratories</u> are <u>great</u>. A lab is the easiest place to <u>control variables</u> so that they're all kept <u>constant</u> (except for the one you're investigating). This makes it easier to carry out a <u>FAIR TEST</u>.

2) For things that you <u>can't investigate in the lab</u> (e.g. climate) you conduct <u>scientific studies</u>. As many of the variables as possible are controlled, to make it a fair test.

3) Old wives' tales, rumours, hearsay, "what someone said", and so on, should be taken with a pinch of salt. Without any evidence they're <u>NOT scientific</u> — they're just <u>opinions</u>.

The <u>Bigger</u> *the* <u>Sample Size</u> *the* <u>Better</u>

1) Data based on <u>small samples</u> isn't as good as data based on large samples. A sample should be <u>representative</u> of the <u>whole population</u> (i.e. it should share as many of the various characteristics in the population as possible) — a small sample can't do that as well.

2) The <u>bigger</u> the sample size the <u>better</u>, but scientists have to be <u>realistic</u> when choosing how big. For example, if you were studying how lifestyle affects people's weight it'd be great to study everyone in the UK (a huge sample), but it'd take ages and cost a bomb. Studying a thousand people is more realistic.

Evidence Needs to be <u>Reliable</u> <u>(Repeatable</u> *and* <u>Reproducible)</u>

Evidence is only <u>reliable</u> if it can be <u>repeated</u> (during an experiment) AND <u>other scientists can reproduce it too</u> (in other experiments). If it's not reliable, you can't believe it.

> RELIABLE means that the data can be <u>repeated, and reproduced by others</u>.

> <u>EXAMPLE:</u> In 1989, two scientists claimed that they'd produced '<u>cold fusion</u>' (the energy source of the Sun — but without the big temperatures). It was huge news — if true, it would have meant free energy for the world... forever. However, other scientists just <u>couldn't reproduce the results</u> — so the results <u>weren't reliable</u>. And until they are, 'cold fusion' isn't going to be accepted as <u>fact</u>.

Evidence Also Needs to Be <u>Valid</u>

> VALID means that the data is <u>reliable</u> AND <u>answers the original question</u>.

> <u>EXAMPLE: DO POWER LINES CAUSE CANCER?</u>
> Some studies have found that children who live near <u>overhead power lines</u> are more likely to develop <u>cancer</u>. What they'd actually found was a <u>correlation</u> (relationship) between the variables "<u>presence of power lines</u>" and "<u>incidence of cancer</u>" — they found that as one changed, so did the other. But this evidence is <u>not enough</u> to say that the power lines <u>cause</u> cancer, as other explanations might be possible. For example, power lines are often near <u>busy roads</u>, so the areas tested could contain <u>different levels</u> of <u>pollution</u> from traffic. So these studies don't show a definite link and so don't <u>answer the original question</u>.

<u>RRRR — Remember, Reliable means Repeatable and Reproducible...</u>

By now you should have realised how <u>important</u> trustworthy <u>evidence</u> is (even more important than a good supply of spot cream). Unfortunately, you need to know loads more about fair tests and experiments — see p. 5-10.

Bias and Issues Created by Science

It isn't all hunky-dory in the world of science — there are some problems...

Scientific Evidence can be Presented in a Biased Way

1) People who want to make a point can sometimes present data in a biased way, e.g. they overemphasise a relationship in the data. (Sometimes without knowing they're doing it.)

2) And there are all sorts of reasons why people might want to do this — for example...

- They want to keep the organisation or company that's funding the research happy. (If the results aren't what they'd like they might not give them any more money to fund further research.)
- Governments might want to persuade voters, other governments, journalists, etc.
- Companies might want to 'big up' their products. Or make impressive safety claims.
- Environmental campaigners might want to persuade people to behave differently.

Things can Affect How Seriously Evidence is Taken

1) If an investigation is done by a team of highly-regarded scientists it's sometimes taken more seriously than evidence from less well known scientists.

2) But having experience, authority or a fancy qualification doesn't necessarily mean the evidence is good — the only way to tell is to look at the evidence scientifically (e.g. is it reliable, valid, etc.).

3) Also, some evidence might be ignored if it could create political problems, or emphasised if it helps a particular cause.

EXAMPLE: Some governments were pretty slow to accept the fact that human activities are causing global warming, despite all the evidence. This is because accepting it means they've got to do something about it, which costs money and could hurt their economy. This could lose them a lot of votes.

Scientific Developments are Great, but they can Raise Issues

Scientific knowledge is increased by doing experiments. And this knowledge leads to scientific developments, e.g. new technologies or new advice. These developments can create issues though. For example:

Economic issues: Society can't always afford to do things scientists recommend (e.g. investing heavily in alternative energy sources) without cutting back elsewhere.

Social issues: Decisions based on scientific evidence affect people — e.g. should fossil fuels be taxed more highly (to invest in alternative energy)? Should alcohol be banned (to prevent health problems)? Would the effect on people's lifestyles be acceptable...

Environmental issues: Chemical fertilisers may help us produce more food — but they also cause environmental problems.

Ethical issues: There are a lot of things that scientific developments have made possible, but should we do them? E.g. clone humans, develop better nuclear weapons.

Trust me — I've got a BSc, PhD, PC, TV and a DVD...

We all tend to swoon at people in authority, but you have to ignore that fact and look at the evidence (just because someone has got a whacking great list of letters after their name doesn't mean the evidence is good). Spotting biased evidence isn't the easiest thing in the world — ask yourself 'Does the scientist (or the person writing about it) stand to gain something (or lose something)?' If they do, it's possible that it could be biased.

Science Has Limits

Science can give us amazing things — cures for diseases, space travel, heated toilet seats...
But science has its limitations — there are questions that it just can't answer.

Some Questions Are Unanswered by Science — So Far

1) We don't understand everything. And we never will. We'll find out more, for sure — as more hypotheses are suggested, and more experiments are done. But there'll always be stuff we don't know.

> EXAMPLES:
> - Today we don't know as much as we'd like about the impacts of global warming.
>   How much will sea level rise? And to what extent will weather patterns change?
> - We also don't know anywhere near as much as we'd like about the Universe.
>   Are there other life forms out there? And what is the Universe made of?

2) These are complicated questions. At the moment scientists don't all agree on the answers because there isn't enough reliable and valid evidence.

3) But eventually, we probably will be able to answer these questions once and for all...
All we need is more evidence.

4) But by then there'll be loads of new questions to answer.

Other Questions Are Unanswerable by Science

1) Then there's the other type... questions that all the experiments in the world won't help us answer — the "Should we be doing this at all?" type questions. There are always two sides...

2) Think about new drugs which can be taken to boost your 'brain power'.

3) Different people have different opinions on them:

> Some people think they're good... Or at least no worse than taking vitamins or eating oily fish. They could let you keep thinking for longer, or improve your memory. It's thought that new drugs could allow people to think in ways that are beyond the powers of normal brains — in effect, to become geniuses...
>
> Other people say they're bad... taking them would give you an unfair advantage in exams, say. And perhaps people would be pressured into taking them so that they could work more effectively, and for longer hours.

4) The question of whether something is morally or ethically right or wrong can't be answered by more experiments — there is no "right" or "wrong" answer.

5) The best we can do is get a consensus from society — a judgement that most people are more or less happy to live by. Science can provide more information to help people make this judgement, and the judgement might change over time. But in the end it's up to people and their conscience.

Chips or rice? — totally unanswerable by science...

Right — get this straight in your head — science can't tell you whether you should or shouldn't do something. That kind of thing is up to you and society to decide. There are tons of questions that science might be able to answer in the future — like how much sea level might rise due to global warming, what the Universe is made of and whatever happened to those pink stripy socks with Santa on that I used to have.

Designing Investigations

Dig out your lab coat and dust down your badly-scratched safety goggles... it's investigation time.
You need to know a shed load about <u>investigations</u> for your <u>controlled assessment</u> and <u>all your exams</u>.
Investigations include <u>experiments</u> and <u>studies</u>. The next six pages take you from start to finish. Enjoy.

Investigations *Produce Evidence* to *Support* or *Disprove* a *Hypothesis*

1) Scientists <u>observe</u> things and come up with <u>hypotheses</u> to explain them (see page 1).

2) To figure out whether a hypothesis might be correct or not you need to do an <u>investigation</u> to <u>gather some evidence</u>.

3) The first step is to use the hypothesis to come up with a <u>prediction</u> — a statement about what you <u>think will happen</u> that you can <u>test</u>.

4) For example, if your <u>hypothesis</u> is:

> "Spots are caused by picking your nose too much."

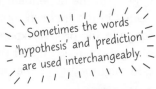
Sometimes the words 'hypothesis' and 'prediction' are used interchangeably.

Then your <u>prediction</u> might be:

> "People who pick their nose more often will have more spots."

5) Investigations are used to see if there are <u>patterns</u> or <u>relationships between two variables</u>. For example, to see if there's a pattern or relationship between the variables 'having spots' and 'nose picking'.

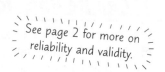
See page 2 for more on reliability and validity.

6) The investigation has to be a <u>FAIR TEST</u> to make sure the evidence is <u>reliable</u> and <u>valid</u>...

To Make an Investigation a *Fair Test* You Have to *Control the Variables*

1) In a lab experiment you usually <u>change one variable</u> and <u>measure</u> how it affects the <u>other variable</u>.

> EXAMPLE: you might change only the temperature of a chemical reaction and measure how this affects the rate of reaction.

2) To make it a fair test <u>everything else</u> that could affect the results should <u>stay the same</u> (otherwise you can't tell if the thing you're changing is causing the results or not — the data won't be reliable or valid).

> EXAMPLE continued: you need to keep the concentration of the reactants the same, otherwise you won't know if any change in the rate of reaction is caused by the change in temperature, or a difference in reactant concentration.

3) The variable you CHANGE is called the INDEPENDENT variable.

4) The variable you MEASURE is called the DEPENDENT variable.

5) The variables that you KEEP THE SAME are called CONTROL variables.

> EXAMPLE continued:
> Independent variable = temperature
> Dependent variable = rate of reaction
> Control variables = concentration of reactants, volume of reactants, etc.

Designing Investigations

Trial Runs help Figure out the Range and Interval of Variable Values

1) It's a good idea to do a trial run first
   — a quick version of your experiment.

2) Trial runs are used to figure out the range of
   variable values used in the proper experiment
   (the upper and lower limit). If you don't get a
   change in the dependent variable at the lower
   values in the trial run, you might narrow the
   range in the proper experiment. But if you
   still get a big change at the upper values
   you might increase the range.

EXAMPLE continued:

- You might do a trial run with a range of
  10-50 °C. If there was no reaction at the lower
  end (e.g. 10-20 °C), you might narrow the
  range to 20-50 °C for the proper experiment.

- If using 1 °C intervals doesn't give you much
  change in the rate of reaction each time
  you might decide to use 5 °C intervals,
  e.g 20, 25, 30, 35, 40, 45, 50 °C...

3) And trial runs can be used to figure out the interval (gaps) between the values too. The intervals can't be
   too small (otherwise the experiment would take ages), or too big (otherwise you might miss something).

4) Trial runs can also help you figure out how many times the experiment has to be repeated to get reliable
   results. E.g. if you repeat it three times and the results are all similar, then three repeats is enough.

It Can Be Hard to Control the Variables in a Study

It's important that a study is a fair test, just like a lab experiment. It's a lot trickier to control the variables in a
study than it is in a lab experiment though (see previous page). Sometimes you can't control them all, but you
can use a control group to help. This is a group of whatever you're studying (people, plants, lemmings, etc.)
that's kept under the same conditions as the group in the experiment, but doesn't have anything done to it.

EXAMPLE: If you're studying the effect of pesticides on crop growth, pesticide is applied to one field
but not to another field (the control field). Both fields are planted with the same crop, and are in the
same area (so they get the same weather conditions). The control field is there to try and account
for variables like the weather, which don't stay the same all the time, but could affect the results.

Investigations Can be Hazardous

1) A hazard is something that can potentially cause harm. Hazards include:

- Microorganisms, e.g. some bacteria can make you ill.
- Chemicals, e.g. sulfuric acid can burn your skin
  and alcohols catch fire easily.
- Fire, e.g. an unattended Bunsen burner is a fire hazard.
- Electricity, e.g. faulty electrical equipment could give you a shock.

Hmm... Where did my
bacteria sample go?

2) Scientists need to manage the risk of hazards by doing things to reduce them. For example:

- If you're working with sulfuric acid, always wear gloves and safety goggles.
  This will reduce the risk of the acid coming into contact with your skin and eyes.

- If you're using a Bunsen burner, stand it on a heat proof mat.
  This will reduce the risk of starting a fire.

You can find out about potential hazards
by looking in textbooks, doing some
internet research, or asking your teacher.

You won't get a trial run at the exam, so get learnin'...

All this info needs to be firmly lodged in your memory. Learn the names of the different variables — if you
remember that the variable you chaNge is called the iNdependent variable, you can figure out the other ones.

Collecting Data

After designing an investigation that's so beautiful people will marvel at it for years to come, you'll need to get your hands mucky and <u>collect some data</u>.

Your Data Should be as *Reliable, Accurate* and *Precise* as Possible

1) To <u>improve</u> reliability you need to <u>repeat</u> the readings and calculate the <u>mean</u> (average). You need to repeat each reading at least <u>three times</u>.

2) To make sure your results are reliable you can cross check them by taking a <u>second set of readings</u> with <u>another instrument</u> (or a <u>different observer</u>).

3) Checking your results match with <u>secondary sources</u>, e.g. other studies, also increases the reliability of your data.

4) Your data also needs to be ACCURATE. Really accurate results are those that are <u>really close</u> to the <u>true answer</u>.

5) Your data also needs to be PRECISE. Precise results are ones where the data is <u>all really close</u> to the <u>mean</u> (i.e. not spread out).

Repeat	Data set 1	Data set 2
1	12	11
2	14	17
3	13	14
Mean	13	14

Data set 1 is more precise than data set 2.

Your *Equipment* has to be *Right for the Job*

1) The measuring equipment you use has to be <u>sensitive enough</u> to measure the changes you're looking for. For example, if you need to measure changes of 1 ml you need to use a measuring cylinder that can measure in 1 ml steps — it'd be no good trying with one that only measures 10 ml steps.

2) The <u>smallest change</u> a measuring instrument can <u>detect</u> is called its RESOLUTION. E.g. some mass balances have a resolution of 1 g, some have a resolution of 0.1 g, and some are even more sensitive.

3) Also, equipment needs to be <u>calibrated</u> so that your data is <u>more accurate</u>. E.g. mass balances need to be set to zero before you start weighing things.

You Need to Look out for *Errors* and *Anomalous Results*

1) The results of your experiment will always <u>vary a bit</u> because of <u>random errors</u> — tiny differences caused by things like <u>human errors</u> in <u>measuring</u>.

2) You can <u>reduce</u> their effect by taking many readings and calculating the <u>mean</u>.

3) If the <u>same error</u> is made every time, it's called a SYSTEMATIC ERROR. For example, if you measured from the very end of your ruler instead of from the 0 cm mark every time, all your measurements would be a bit small.

Repeating the experiment in the exact same way and calculating an average won't correct a systematic error.

4) Just to make things more complicated, if a systematic error is caused by using <u>equipment</u> that <u>isn't calibrated properly</u> it's called a ZERO ERROR. For example, if a mass balance always reads 1 gram before you put anything on it, all your measurements will be 1 gram too heavy.

5) You can <u>compensate</u> for some systematic errors if you know about them though, e.g. if your mass balance always reads 1 gram before you put anything on it you can subtract 1 gram from all your results.

6) Sometimes you get a result that <u>doesn't seem to fit in</u> with the rest at all.

7) These results are called ANOMALOUS RESULTS.

8) You should investigate them and try to <u>work out what happened</u>. If you can work out what happened (e.g. you measured something totally wrong) you can <u>ignore</u> them when processing your results.

Park	Number of pigeons	Number of crazy tramps
A	28	1
B	42	2
C	1127	0

Zero error — sounds like a Bruce Willis film...

Weirdly, data can be really <u>precise</u> but <u>not very accurate</u>, e.g. a fancy piece of lab equipment might give results that are precise, but if it's not calibrated properly those results won't be accurate.

Processing and Presenting Data

After you've collected your data you'll have <u>oodles of info</u> that you have to <u>make some kind of sense of</u>. You need to <u>process</u> and <u>present</u> it so you can look for <u>patterns</u> and <u>relationships</u> in it.

Data **Needs to be** Organised

1) Tables are dead useful for <u>organising data</u>.

2) When you draw a table <u>use a ruler</u>, make sure <u>each column</u> has a <u>heading</u> (including the <u>units</u>) and keep it neat and tidy.

3) Annoyingly, tables are about as useful as a chocolate teapot for showing <u>patterns</u> or <u>relationships</u> in data. You need to use some kind of graph for that.

You Might Have to Process Your Data

1) When you've done repeats of an experiment you should always calculate the <u>mean</u> (average). To do this <u>ADD TOGETHER</u> all the data values and <u>DIVIDE</u> by the total number of values in the sample.

2) You might also need to calculate the <u>range</u> (how spread out the data is). To do this find the <u>LARGEST</u> number and <u>SUBTRACT</u> the <u>SMALLEST</u> number from it.

Ignore anomalous results when calculating these.

EXAMPLE

Test tube	Repeat 1 (g)	Repeat 2 (g)	Repeat 3 (g)	Mean (g)	Range (g)
A	28	37	32	(28 + 37 + 32) ÷ 3 = 32.3	37 − 28 = 9
B	47	51	60	(47 + 51 + 60) ÷ 3 = 52.7	60 − 47 = 13
C	68	72	70	(68 + 72 + 70) ÷ 3 = 70.0	72 − 68 = 4

If Your Data Comes in Categories, **Present It in a** Bar Chart

1) If the independent variable is <u>categoric</u> (comes in distinct categories, e.g. blood types, metals) you should use a <u>bar chart</u> to display the data.

2) You also use them if the independent variable is <u>discrete</u> (the data can be counted in chunks, where there's no in-between value, e.g. number of people is discrete because you can't have half a person).

3) There are some <u>golden rules</u> you need to follow for <u>drawing</u> bar charts:

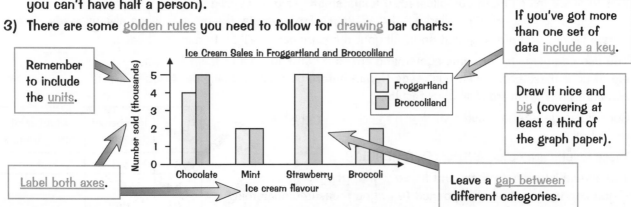

Remember to include the <u>units</u>.

<u>Label both axes.</u>

If you've got more than one set of data <u>include a key</u>.

Draw it nice and <u>big</u> (covering at least a third of the graph paper).

Leave a <u>gap between</u> different categories.

Discrete variables love bar charts — although they'd never tell anyone that...

The stuff on this page might all seem a bit basic, but it's <u>easy marks</u> in the exams (which you'll kick yourself if you don't get). Examiners are a bit picky when it comes to bar charts — if you don't draw them properly they won't be happy. Also, <u>double check</u> any mean or range <u>calculations</u> you do, just to be sure they're correct.

Presenting Data

Scientists just <u>love</u> presenting data as <u>line graphs</u> (weirdos)...

If Your Data is Continuous, Plot a Line Graph

1) If the independent variable is <u>continuous</u> (numerical data that can have any value within a range, e.g. length, volume, temperature) you should use a <u>line graph</u> to display the data.

2) Here are the <u>rules</u> for <u>drawing</u> line graphs:

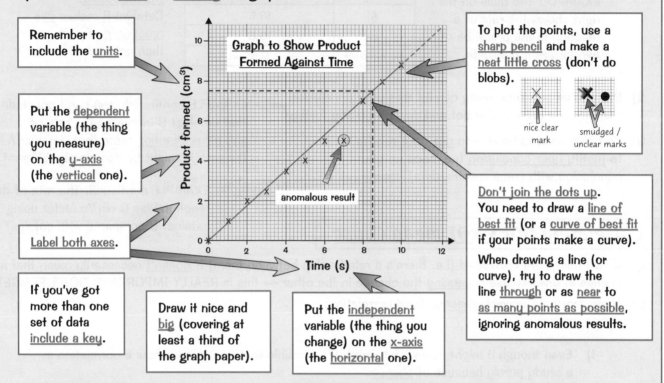

Remember to include the <u>units</u>.

Put the <u>dependent</u> variable (the thing you measure) on the <u>y-axis</u> (the <u>vertical</u> one).

<u>Label both axes</u>.

If you've got more than one set of data <u>include a key</u>.

Draw it nice and <u>big</u> (covering at least a third of the graph paper).

Put the <u>independent</u> variable (the thing you change) on the <u>x-axis</u> (the <u>horizontal</u> one).

To plot the points, use a <u>sharp pencil</u> and make a <u>neat little cross</u> (don't do blobs).

nice clear mark — smudged / unclear marks

<u>Don't join the dots up</u>. You need to draw a <u>line of best fit</u> (or a <u>curve of best fit</u> if your points make a curve).

When drawing a line (or curve), try to draw the line <u>through</u> or as <u>near</u> to <u>as many points as possible</u>, ignoring anomalous results.

Graph to Show Product Formed Against Time

Product formed (cm³) / Time (s)

anomalous result

3) Line graphs are used to <u>show the relationship</u> between two variables (just like other graphs).

4) Data can show <u>three</u> different types of correlation (relationship):

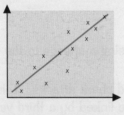

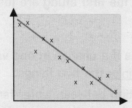

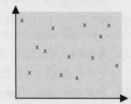

<u>POSITIVE</u> <u>correlation</u> — as one variable <u>increases</u> the other <u>increases</u>.

<u>NEGATIVE</u> <u>correlation</u> — as one variable <u>increases</u> the other <u>decreases</u>.

<u>NO correlation</u> — there's <u>no relationship</u> between the two variables.

5) You need to be able to describe the following relationships on line graphs too:

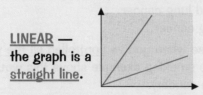

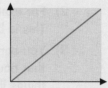

<u>LINEAR</u> — the graph is a <u>straight line</u>.

<u>DIRECTLY PROPORTIONAL</u> — the graph is a <u>straight line</u> where both variables increase (or decrease) in the <u>same ratio</u>.

There's a positive correlation between revision and boredom...

...but there's also a positive correlation between <u>revision</u> and getting a <u>better mark in the exam</u>. Cover the page and write down the <u>eight things</u> you need to remember when <u>drawing graphs</u>. No sneaky peeking either — I saw you.

Drawing Conclusions

Congratulations — you've made it to the final step of a gruelling investigation — drawing conclusions.

You Can Only Conclude What the Data Shows and NO MORE

1) Drawing conclusions might seem pretty straightforward — you just look at your data and say what pattern or relationship you see between the dependent and independent variables.

EXAMPLE: The table on the right shows the rate of a reaction in the presence of two different catalysts.

Catalyst	Rate of reaction (cm³/s)
A	13.5
B	19.5
No catalyst	5.5

CONCLUSION: Catalyst B makes this reaction go faster than catalyst A.

2) But you've got to be really careful that your conclusion matches the data you've got and doesn't go any further.

EXAMPLE continued: You can't conclude that catalyst B increases the rate of any other reaction more than catalyst A — the results might be completely different.

3) You also need to be able to use your results to justify your conclusion (i.e. back up your conclusion with some specific data).

EXAMPLE continued: The rate of this reaction was 6 cm³/s faster using catalyst B compared with catalyst A.

Correlation DOES NOT mean Cause

1) If two things are correlated (i.e. there's a relationship between them) it doesn't necessarily mean that a change in one variable is causing the change in the other — this is REALLY IMPORTANT, DON'T FORGET IT.

2) There are three possible reasons for a correlation:

① CHANCE

1) Even though it might seem a bit weird, it's possible that two things show a correlation in a study purely because of chance.

2) For example, one study might find a correlation between people's hair colour and how good they are at frisbee. But other scientists don't get a correlation when they investigate it — the results of the first study are just a fluke.

② LINKED BY A 3rd VARIABLE

1) A lot of the time it may look as if a change in one variable is causing a change in the other, but it isn't — a third variable links the two things.

2) For example, there's a correlation between water temperature and shark attacks. This obviously isn't because warmer water makes sharks crazy. Instead, they're linked by a third variable — the number of people swimming (more people swim when the water's hotter, and with more people in the water you get more shark attacks).

③ CAUSE

1) Sometimes a change in one variable does cause a change in the other.

2) For example, there's a correlation between smoking and lung cancer. This is because chemicals in tobacco smoke cause lung cancer.

3) You can only conclude that a correlation is due to cause when you've controlled all the variables that could, just could, be affecting the result. (For the smoking example above this would include things like age and exposure to other things that cause cancer).

I conclude that this page is a bit dull...

...although, just because I find it dull doesn't mean that I can conclude it's dull (you might think it's the most interesting thing since that kid got his head stuck in the railings near school). In the exams you could be given a conclusion and asked whether some data supports it — so make sure you understand how far conclusions can go.

Controlled Assessment (ISA)

Controlled Assessment involves <u>doing an experiment</u> and <u>answering two question papers on it</u> under exam conditions. Sounds thrilling.

There are Two Sections in the Controlled Assessment

(1) Planning

Before you do the Section 1 question paper you'll be given time to do some <u>research</u> into the topic that's been set — you'll need to develop a <u>hypothesis/prediction</u> and come up with <u>two</u> different methods to test it. In your research, you should use a variety of <u>different sources</u> (e.g. the internet, textbooks etc.). You'll need to be able to <u>outline both methods</u> and say which one is <u>best</u> (and why it's the best one) and describe your preferred method in <u>detail</u>. You're allowed to write <u>notes</u> about your two methods on <u>one side of A4</u> and have them with you for both question papers. In Section 1, you could be asked things like:

1) What your <u>hypothesis/prediction</u> is.
2) What variables you're going to <u>control</u> (and <u>how</u> you're going to control them).
3) What <u>measurements</u> you're going to take.
4) What <u>range</u> and <u>interval</u> of values you will use for the <u>independent variable</u>.
5) How you'd figure out the range and interval using a <u>trial run</u> (sometimes called a 'preliminary investigation' in the question papers). See page 6 for more.
6) How many times you're going to <u>repeat</u> the experiment — a minimum of <u>three</u> is a good idea.
7) What <u>equipment</u> you're going to use (and <u>why</u> that equipment is <u>right for the job</u>).
8) <u>How to carry out</u> the experiment, i.e. what you do first, what you do second...
9) What <u>hazards</u> are involved in doing the experiment, and <u>how to reduce them</u>.
10) What <u>table</u> you'll draw to put your results in. See page 8 for how to draw one that examiners will love.

There's lots of help on all of these things on pages 5-10.

When you've done the planning and completed the first question paper you'll actually <u>do the experiment</u>. Then you'll have to <u>present your data</u>. Make sure you use the <u>right type of graph</u>, and you <u>draw it properly</u> — see pages 8-9 for help. After that it's onto the Section 2 question paper...

(2) Drawing Conclusions and Evaluating

For the Section 2 question paper you have to do these things for <u>your experiment</u>:

1) <u>Analyse</u> and <u>draw conclusions</u> from your results. For this you need to <u>describe the relationship</u> between the variables in <u>detail</u> — see the previous page for how to do this. E.g. 'I found that there is a relationship between picking your nose and having spots. The more often you pick your nose the more spots you'll have. For example, my results showed...'.

2) Say whether your results <u>back up the hypothesis/prediction</u>, and give reasons <u>why</u> or <u>why not</u>. E.g. 'My results did not back up the prediction. The prediction was that picking your nose more has no effect on the number of spots you have. But I found the opposite to be true in my investigation'.

3) <u>Evaluate</u> your experiment. For this you need to <u>suggest ways you could improve your experiment</u>.
   - Comment on your <u>equipment</u> and <u>method</u>, e.g. could you have used more <u>accurate</u> equipment?
   - Make sure you <u>explain how</u> the improvements would give you <u>better data</u> next time.
   - <u>Refer to your results</u>. E.g. 'My data wasn't accurate enough because the mass balance I used only measured in 1 g steps. I could use a more sensitive one next time (e.g. a mass balance that measures in 0.5 g steps) to get more accurate data'.

You'll also be <u>given some secondary data</u> (data collected by someone else) from an experiment on the same topic and asked to <u>analyse it</u>. This just involves doing what you did for your data with the secondary data, e.g. draw conclusions from it.

If that's controlled assessment, I'd hate to see uncontrolled assessment...

That might be an Everest-sized list of stuff, but it's <u>all important</u>. No need to panic at the sight of it though — as long as you've <u>learnt everything</u> on the previous few pages, you should be fine.

Atoms and Elements

Atoms are the building blocks of <u>everything</u> — and I mean everything.
They're <u>amazingly tiny</u> — you can only see them with an incredibly powerful microscope.

Atoms have a Small <u>Nucleus</u> Surrounded by <u>Electrons</u>

There are quite a few different (and equally useful) models of the atom — but chemists tend to like this <u>nuclear model</u> best. You can use it to explain pretty much the whole of Chemistry... which is nice.

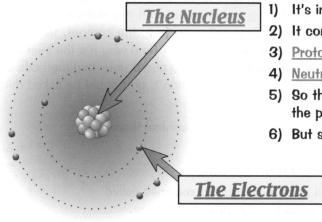

The Nucleus

1) It's in the <u>middle</u> of the atom.
2) It contains <u>protons</u> and <u>neutrons</u>.
3) <u>Protons</u> are <u>positively charged</u>.
4) <u>Neutrons</u> have <u>no charge</u> (they're neutral).
5) So the nucleus has a <u>positive charge</u> overall because of the protons.
6) But size-wise it's <u>tiny</u> compared to the rest of the atom.

The Electrons

1) Move <u>around</u> the nucleus.
2) They're <u>negatively charged</u>.
3) They're <u>tiny</u>, but they cover <u>a lot of space</u>.
4) They occupy <u>shells</u> around the nucleus.
5) These shells explain <u>the whole of Chemistry</u>.

Number of Protons <u>Equals</u> Number of Electrons

1) Atoms have <u>no charge</u> overall. They are neutral.
2) The <u>charge</u> on the electrons is the <u>same</u> size as the charge on the <u>protons</u> — but <u>opposite</u>.
3) This means the <u>number</u> of <u>protons</u> always equals the <u>number</u> of <u>electrons</u> in an <u>atom</u>.
4) If some electrons are <u>added or removed</u>, the atom becomes <u>charged</u> and is then an <u>ion</u>.

Elements <u>Consist of</u> One Type <u>of Atom Only</u>

1) Atoms can have different numbers of protons, neutrons and electrons.
   It's the number of <u>protons</u> in the nucleus that decides what <u>type</u> of atom it is.
2) For example, an atom with <u>one proton</u> in its nucleus is <u>hydrogen</u> and an atom with <u>two protons</u> is <u>helium</u>.
3) If a substance only contains <u>one type</u> of atom it's called an <u>element</u>.
4) There are about <u>100 different elements</u> — quite a lot of everyday substances are elements:

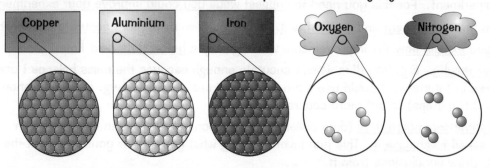

So <u>all the atoms</u> of a particular <u>element</u> (e.g. nitrogen) have the <u>same number</u> of protons...

...and <u>different elements</u> have atoms with <u>different numbers</u> of protons.

<u>Number of protons = number of electrons...</u>

This stuff might seem a bit useless at first, but it should be permanently engraved into your mind.
You need to <u>know these basic facts</u> — then you'll have a better chance of understanding the rest of Chemistry.

The Periodic Table

Chemistry would be <u>really messy</u> if it was all <u>big lists</u> of names and properties. So instead they've come up with a kind of <u>shorthand</u> for the names, and made a beautiful table to organise the elements — like a big <u>filing system</u>. Might not be much fun, but it makes life (and <u>exam questions</u>) much, much <u>easier</u>.

Atoms Can be Represented by Symbols

Atoms of each element can be represented by a <u>one or two letter symbol</u> — it's a type of <u>shorthand</u> that saves you the bother of having to write the full name of the element.

Some make <u>perfect sense</u>, e.g.

| C = carbon | O = oxygen | Mg = magnesium |

Others seem to make about as much sense as an apple with a handle.

E.g. | Na = sodium | Fe = iron | Pb = lead |

Most of these odd symbols actually come from the Latin names of the elements.

The Periodic Table Puts Elements with Similar Properties Together

1) The periodic table is laid out so that elements with <u>similar properties</u> form <u>columns</u>.

2) These <u>vertical columns</u> are called <u>groups</u> and Roman numerals are often used for them.

3) All of the elements in a <u>group</u> have the <u>same number</u> of <u>electrons</u> in their <u>outer shell</u>.

4) This is why <u>elements</u> in the same group have <u>similar properties</u>. So, if you know the <u>properties</u> of <u>one element</u>, you can <u>predict</u> properties of <u>other elements</u> in that group.

5) For example, the <u>Group 1</u> elements are Li, Na, K, Rb, Cs and Fr. They're all <u>metals</u> and they <u>react the same way</u>. E.g. they all react with water to form an <u>alkaline solution</u> and <u>hydrogen gas</u>, and they all react with oxygen to form an <u>oxide</u>.

6) The elements in the final column (<u>Group 0</u>) are the noble gases. They all have <u>eight electrons</u> in their <u>outer shell</u>, apart from helium (which has two). This means that they're <u>stable</u> and <u>unreactive</u>.

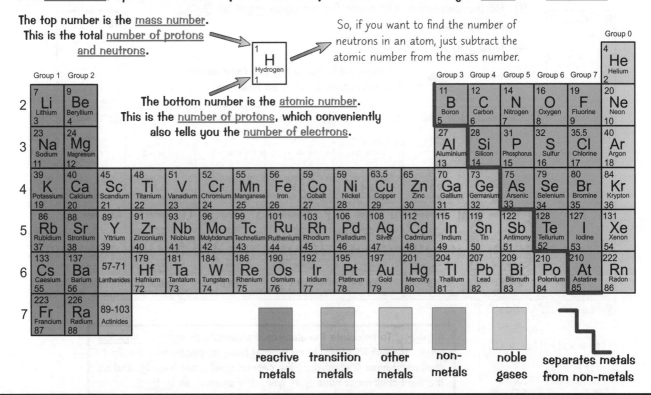

The top number is the <u>mass number</u>. This is the total <u>number of protons and neutrons</u>.

So, if you want to find the number of neutrons in an atom, just subtract the atomic number from the mass number.

The bottom number is the <u>atomic number</u>. This is the <u>number of protons</u>, which conveniently also tells you the <u>number of electrons</u>.

reactive metals   transition metals   other metals   non-metals   noble gases   separates metals from non-metals

I'm in a chemistry band — I play the symbols...

Scientists keep making <u>new elements</u> and feeling well chuffed with themselves. The trouble is, these new elements only last for <u>a fraction of a second</u> before falling apart. You <u>don't</u> need to know the properties of each group of the periodic table, but if you're told, for example, that fluorine (Group 7) forms <u>two-atom molecules</u>, it's a fair guess that chlorine, bromine, iodine and astatine <u>do too</u>.

Electron Shells

The fact that electrons occupy "shells" around the nucleus is what causes the whole of chemistry. Remember that, and watch how it applies to each bit of it. It's ace.

Electron Shell Rules:

1) Electrons always occupy shells (sometimes called energy levels).

2) The lowest energy levels are always filled first — these are the ones closest to the nucleus.

3) Only a certain number of electrons are allowed in each shell:
   1st shell: 2   2nd shell: 8   3rd shell: 8

4) Atoms are much happier when they have full electron shells — like the noble gases in Group 0.

5) In most atoms the outer shell is not full and this makes the atom want to react to fill it.

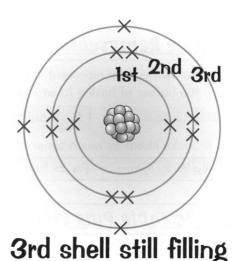

1st 2nd 3rd

3rd shell still filling

Follow the Rules to Work Out Electronic Structures

You need to know the electronic structures for the first 20 elements (things get a bit more complicated after that). But they're not hard to work out. For a quick example, take nitrogen. Follow the steps...

1) The periodic table tells us nitrogen has seven protons... so it must have seven electrons.

2) Follow the 'Electron Shell Rules' above. The first shell can only take 2 electrons and the second shell can take a maximum of 8 electrons.

3) So the electronic structure for nitrogen must be 2, 5. Easy peasy.

4) Now you try it for argon.

The periodic table has a big gap here where the transition metals fit in on row four.

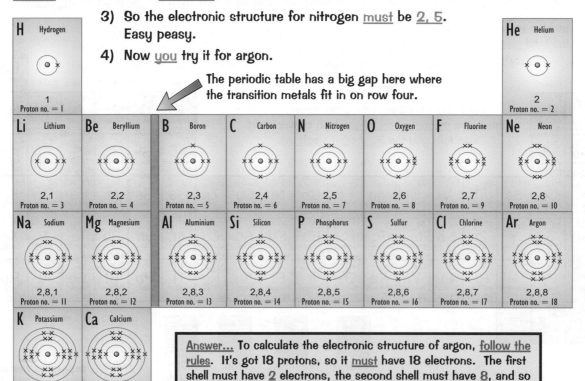

Answer... To calculate the electronic structure of argon, follow the rules. It's got 18 protons, so it must have 18 electrons. The first shell must have 2 electrons, the second shell must have 8, and so the third shell must have 8 as well. It's as easy as 2, 8, 8.

One little duck and two fat ladies — 2, 8, 8...

You need to know enough about electron shells to draw out that whole diagram at the bottom of the page without looking at it. Obviously, you don't have to learn each element separately, just learn the pattern. Cover the page: using a periodic table, find the atom with the electron structure 2, 8, 6.

Compounds

Life'd be oh so simple if you only had to worry about elements, even if there are a hundred or so of them. But you can mix and match elements to make lots of compounds, which complicates things no end.

Atoms Join Together to Make Compounds

1) When <u>different elements react</u>, atoms form <u>chemical bonds</u> with other atoms to form <u>compounds</u>. It's <u>usually difficult</u> to <u>separate</u> the two original elements out again.

2) <u>Making bonds</u> involves atoms giving away, taking or sharing <u>electrons</u>. Only the <u>electrons</u> are involved — it's nothing to do with the nuclei of the atoms at all.

3) A compound which is formed from a <u>metal</u> and a <u>non-metal</u> consists of <u>ions</u>. The <u>metal</u> atoms <u>lose</u> electrons to form <u>positive ions</u> and the non-metal atoms <u>gain</u> electrons to form <u>negative ions</u>. The <u>opposite charges</u> (positive and negative) of the ions mean that they're strongly <u>attracted</u> to each other. This is called <u>IONIC bonding</u>.

   E.g. NaCl

   Na   Cl   A sodium atom <u>gives</u> an electron to a chlorine atom.

4) A compound formed from <u>non-metals</u> consists of <u>molecules</u>. Each atom <u>shares</u> an <u>electron</u> with another atom — this is called a <u>COVALENT</u> bond. Each atom has to make enough covalent bonds to <u>fill up</u> its <u>outer shell</u>.

   E.g. HCl

   H Cl   A hydrogen atom bonds with a chlorine atom by <u>sharing</u> an electron with it.

5) The <u>properties</u> of a compound are <u>totally different</u> from the properties of the <u>original elements</u>. For example, if iron (a lustrous magnetic metal) and sulfur (a nice yellow powder) react, the compound formed (<u>iron sulfide</u>) is a <u>dull grey solid lump</u>, and doesn't behave <u>anything like</u> either iron or sulfur.

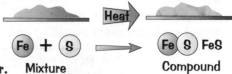

Heat

Fe + S   Fe S FeS
Mixture   Compound

6) Compounds can be <u>small molecules</u> like water, or <u>great whopping lattices</u> like sodium chloride (when I say whopping I'm talking in atomic terms).

   O H a water
   H   molecule

Part of a sodium chloride lattice
● sodium ion
● chloride ion

A Formula Shows What Atoms are in a Compound

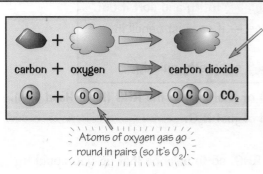

carbon + oxygen ⟹ carbon dioxide

C + O O ⟹ O C O CO$_2$

Atoms of oxygen gas go round in pairs (so it's O$_2$).

1) Carbon dioxide, CO_2, is a <u>compound</u> formed from a <u>chemical reaction</u> between carbon and oxygen. It contains <u>1 carbon atom</u> and <u>2 oxygen atoms</u>.

2) Here's another example: the formula of <u>sulfuric acid</u> is H_2SO_4. So, each molecule contains <u>2 hydrogen atoms</u>, <u>1 sulfur atom</u> and <u>4 oxygen atoms</u>.

3) There might be <u>brackets</u> in a formula, e.g. calcium hydroxide is $Ca(OH)_2$. The little number outside the bracket applies to <u>everything</u> inside the brackets. So in $Ca(OH)_2$ there is <u>1 calcium atom</u>, <u>2 oxygen atoms</u> and <u>2 hydrogen atoms</u>.

Not learning this stuff will only compound your problems...

So, it turns out that <u>atoms</u> can be very caring and <u>sharing</u> little things when it comes to <u>forming compounds</u>. In fact, I know some people who could learn a lot from them. In fact, just the other day... Anyway, enough of my problems. Make sure you understand <u>what compounds are</u> and what the <u>difference</u> is between <u>covalent</u> and <u>ionic</u> bonding. It'll come in incredibly useful later on in your chemistry learnings. I promise.

Balancing Equations

Equations need a lot of practice if you're going to get them right — don't just skate over this stuff.

Atoms Aren't Lost or Made in Chemical Reactions

1) During chemical reactions, things don't appear out of nowhere and things don't just disappear.

2) You still have the same atoms at the end of a chemical reaction as you had at the start. They're just arranged in different ways.

3) Balanced symbol equations show the atoms at the start (the reactant atoms) and the atoms at the end (the product atoms) and how they're arranged. For example:

Word equation: magnesium + oxygen → magnesium oxide
Balanced symbol equation: 2Mg + O$_2$ → 2MgO

4) Because atoms aren't gained or lost, the mass of the reactants equals the mass of the products. So, if you completely react 6 g of magnesium with 4 g of oxygen, you'd end up with 10 g of magnesium oxide.

Balancing the Equation — Match Them Up One by One

1) There must always be the same number of atoms of each element on both sides — they can't just disappear.

2) You balance the equation by putting numbers in front of the formulas where needed. Take this equation for reacting sulfuric acid (H_2SO_4) with sodium hydroxide (NaOH) to get sodium sulfate (Na_2SO_4) and water (H_2O):

$$H_2SO_4 + NaOH \rightarrow Na_2SO_4 + H_2O$$

The formulas are all correct but the numbers of some atoms don't match up on both sides. E.g. there are 3 Hs on the left, but only 2 on the right. You can't change formulas like H_2O to H_3O. You can only put numbers in front of them:

Method: Balance Just ONE Type of Atom at a Time

The more you practise, the quicker you get, but all you do is this:

1) Find an element that doesn't balance and pencil in a number to try and sort it out.

2) See where it gets you. It may create another imbalance — if so, just pencil in another number and see where that gets you.

3) Carry on chasing unbalanced elements and it'll sort itself out pretty quickly.

I'll show you. In the equation above you soon notice we're short of H atoms on the RHS (Right-Hand Side).

1) The only thing you can do about that is make it $2H_2O$ instead of just H_2O:
$$H_2SO_4 + NaOH \rightarrow Na_2SO_4 + 2H_2O$$

2) But that now causes too many H atoms and O atoms on the RHS, so to balance that up you could try putting 2NaOH on the LHS (Left-Hand Side):
$$H_2SO_4 + 2NaOH \rightarrow Na_2SO_4 + 2H_2O$$

3) And suddenly there it is! Everything balances. And you'll notice the Na just sorted itself out.

Balancing equations — weigh it up in your mind...

REMEMBER WHAT THOSE NUMBERS MEAN: A number in front of a formula applies to the entire formula. So, $3Na_2SO_4$ means three lots of Na_2SO_4. The little numbers in the middle or at the end of a formula only apply to the atom or brackets immediately before. So the 4 in Na_2SO_4 just means 4 Os, not 4 Ss.

Using Limestone

Limestone's often formed from <u>sea shells</u>, so you might not expect that it'd be useful as a <u>building material</u>...

Limestone *is Mainly* Calcium Carbonate

Limestone's <u>quarried</u> out of the ground — it's great for making into <u>blocks</u> for building with. Fine old buildings like <u>cathedrals</u> are often made purely from limestone blocks. It's pretty <u>sturdy</u> stuff, but don't go thinking it doesn't <u>react</u> with anything.

St Paul's Cathedral is made from limestone.

1) Limestone is mainly <u>calcium carbonate</u> — $CaCO_3$.

2) When it's heated it <u>thermally decomposes</u> to make <u>calcium oxide</u> and <u>carbon dioxide</u>.

> calcium carbonate → calcium oxide + carbon dioxide
> $$CaCO_{3(s)} \quad \rightarrow \quad CaO_{(s)} \quad + \quad CO_{2(g)}$$

Thermal decomposition is when one substance chemically changes into at least two new substances when it's heated.

- When <u>magnesium</u>, <u>copper</u>, <u>zinc</u> and <u>sodium carbonates</u> are heated, they decompose in the <u>same way</u>. E.g. magnesium carbonate → magnesium oxide + carbon dioxide (i.e. $MgCO_3 \rightarrow MgO + CO_2$)

- However, you might have <u>difficulty</u> doing some of these reactions in class — a <u>Bunsen burner</u> can't reach a <u>high enough temperature</u> to thermally decompose some carbonates of <u>Group I metals</u>.

3) Calcium carbonate also reacts with <u>acid</u> to make a <u>calcium salt</u>, <u>carbon dioxide</u> and <u>water</u>. E.g.:

> calcium carbonate + sulfuric acid → calcium sulfate + carbon dioxide + water
> $$CaCO_3 \quad + \quad H_2SO_4 \quad \rightarrow \quad CaSO_4 \quad + \quad CO_2 \quad + \quad H_2O$$

- The type of <u>salt</u> produced <u>depends</u> on the type of <u>acid</u>. For example, a reaction with <u>hydrochloric</u> acid would make a <u>chloride</u> (e.g. $CaCl_2$).

This reaction means that limestone is damaged by acid rain (see p.28).

- Other carbonates that react with acids are <u>magnesium</u>, <u>copper</u>, <u>zinc</u> and <u>sodium</u>.

Calcium Oxide *Reacts with* Water *to Produce* Calcium Hydroxide

1) When you <u>add water</u> to calcium oxide you get <u>calcium hydroxide</u>.

> calcium oxide + water ⟶ calcium hydroxide   or $CaO + H_2O \longrightarrow Ca(OH)_2$

2) Calcium hydroxide is an <u>alkali</u> which can be used to neutralise <u>acidic soil</u> in fields. Powdered limestone can be used for this too, but the <u>advantage</u> of <u>calcium hydroxide</u> is that it works <u>much faster</u>.

3) Calcium hydroxide can also be used in a <u>test</u> for <u>carbon dioxide</u>. If you make a <u>solution</u> of calcium hydroxide in water (called <u>limewater</u>) and bubble <u>gas</u> through it, the solution will turn <u>cloudy</u> if there's <u>carbon dioxide</u> in the gas. The cloudiness is caused by the formation of <u>calcium carbonate</u>.

> calcium hydroxide + carbon dioxide → calcium carbonate + water
> $$Ca(OH)_2 \quad + \quad CO_2 \quad \rightarrow \quad CaCO_3 \quad + \quad H_2O$$

Limestone *is Used to Make* Other Useful Things *Too*

1) Powdered limestone is <u>heated</u> in a kiln with <u>powdered clay</u> to make <u>cement</u>.

2) Cement can be mixed with <u>sand</u> and <u>water</u> to make <u>mortar</u>. <u>Mortar</u> is the stuff you stick <u>bricks</u> together with. You can also add <u>calcium hydroxide</u> to mortar.

3) Or you can mix cement with <u>sand</u> and <u>aggregate</u> (water and gravel) to make <u>concrete</u>.

Limestone — a sea creature's cementery...

Wow. It sounds like you can achieve <u>pretty much anything</u> with limestone, possibly apart from a bouncy castle. I wonder what we'd be using instead if all those sea creatures hadn't died and conveniently become rock?

Using Limestone

Using limestone ain't all hunky-dory — tearing it out of the ground and making stuff from it causes quite a few <u>problems</u>. You need to learn the problems... And to top it all off you've got to learn the <u>advantages</u> and <u>disadvantages</u> of using limestone, cement and concrete as building materials too. It's just not your day.

Quarrying Limestone Makes a Right Mess of the Landscape

Digging limestone out of the ground can cause environmental problems.

1) For a start, it makes <u>huge ugly holes</u> which permanently change the landscape.

2) <u>Quarrying</u> processes, like blasting rocks apart with explosives, make lots of <u>noise</u> and <u>dust</u> in quiet, scenic areas.

3) Quarrying <u>destroys the habitats</u> of animals and birds.

4) The limestone needs to be <u>transported away</u> from the quarry — usually in lorries. This causes more noise and pollution.

5) Waste materials produce unsightly <u>tips</u>.

Making Stuff from Limestone Causes Pollution Too

1) <u>Cement factories</u> make a lot of <u>dust</u>, which can cause <u>breathing problems</u> for some people.

2) <u>Energy</u> is needed to produce cement and quicklime. The energy is likely to come from burning <u>fossil fuels</u>, which causes pollution.

See page 28 for more on pollution caused by burning fossil fuels.

But on the Plus Side...

1) Limestone provides things that people want — like <u>houses</u> and <u>roads</u>. Chemicals used in making <u>dyes</u>, <u>paints</u> and <u>medicines</u> also come from limestone.

2) Limestone products are used to <u>neutralise acidic soil</u>. Acidity in lakes and rivers caused by <u>acid rain</u> is also <u>neutralised</u> by limestone products.

3) Limestone is also used in power station chimneys to <u>neutralise sulfur dioxide</u>, which is a cause of acid rain.

4) The quarry and associated businesses provide <u>jobs</u> for people and bring more money into the <u>local economy</u>. This can lead to <u>local improvements</u> in transport, roads, recreation facilities and health.

5) Once quarrying is complete, <u>landscaping</u> and <u>restoration</u> of the area is normally required as part of the planning permission.

Limestone Products Have Advantages and Disadvantages

Limestone and concrete (made from cement) are used as <u>building materials</u>.
In some cases they're <u>perfect</u> for the job, but in other cases they're a bit of a compromise.

1) Limestone is <u>widely available</u> and is <u>cheaper</u> than granite or marble. It's also a fairly easy rock to <u>cut</u>.

2) Some limestone is more <u>hard-wearing</u> than marble, but it still looks <u>attractive</u>.

3) Concrete can be poured into <u>moulds</u> to make blocks or panels that can be joined together. It's a <u>very quick and cheap</u> way of constructing buildings — <u>and it shows</u>... — concrete has got to be the most <u>hideously unattractive</u> building material ever known.

4) Limestone, concrete and cement <u>don't rot</u> when they get wet like wood does. They can't be gnawed away by <u>insects</u> or <u>rodents</u> either. And to top it off, they're <u>fire-resistant</u> too.

5) Concrete <u>doesn't corrode</u> like lots of metals do. It does have a fairly <u>low tensile strength</u> though, and can crack. If it's <u>reinforced</u> with steel bars it'll be much stronger.

Tough revision here — this stuff's rock hard...

There's a <u>downside</u> to everything, including using limestone — ripping open huge quarries definitely <u>spoils the countryside</u>. But you have to find a <u>balance</u> between the environmental and ecological factors and the economic and social factors — is it worth keeping the countryside pristine if it means loads of people have nowhere to live because there's no stuff available to build houses with?

Getting Metals from Rocks

A few <u>unreactive metals</u> like <u>gold</u> are found in the Earth as the <u>metal itself</u>, rather than as a compound. The rest of the metals we get by extracting them from rocks — and I bet you're just itching to find out how...

Ores *Contain* Enough Metal *to Make* Extraction *Worthwhile*

1) A <u>metal ore</u> is a <u>rock</u> which contains <u>enough metal</u> to make it <u>worthwhile</u> extracting the metal from it.

2) In many cases the ore is an <u>oxide</u> of the metal. For example, the main <u>aluminium ore</u> is called <u>bauxite</u> — it's aluminium oxide (Al_2O_3).

3) <u>Most metals</u> need to be extracted from their ores using a <u>chemical reaction</u>.

4) The <u>economics</u> (profitability) of metal extraction can <u>change</u> over <u>time</u>. For example:

• If the market <u>price</u> of a metal <u>drops</u> a lot, it <u>might not</u> be worth extracting it. If the <u>price increases</u> a lot then it <u>might be worth</u> extracting <u>more</u> of it.

• As <u>technology improves</u>, it becomes possible to <u>extract more</u> metal from a sample of rock than was originally possible. So it might now be <u>worth</u> extracting metal that <u>wasn't</u> worth extracting <u>in the past</u>.

Metals *Are* Extracted *From their Ores* Chemically

1) A metal can be extracted from its ore <u>chemically</u> — by <u>reduction</u> (see below) or by <u>electrolysis</u> (splitting with electricity, see page 20).

2) Some ores may have to be <u>concentrated</u> before the metal is extracted — this just involves getting rid of the <u>unwanted rocky material</u>.

3) <u>Electrolysis</u> can also be used to <u>purify</u> the extracted metal (see page 20).

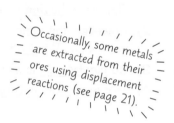

Occasionally, some metals are extracted from their ores using displacement reactions (see page 21).

Some Metals can be *Extracted* by Reduction *with* Carbon

1) A metal can be <u>extracted</u> from its ore chemically by <u>reduction</u> using <u>carbon</u>.

2) When an ore is reduced, <u>oxygen is removed</u> from it, e.g.

$2Fe_2O_3$	+	$3C$	$\rightarrow$	$4Fe$	+	$3CO_2$
iron(III) oxide	+	carbon	$\rightarrow$	iron	+	carbon dioxide

3) The position of the metal in the <u>reactivity series</u> determines whether it can be extracted by <u>reduction</u> with carbon.

a) Metals <u>higher than carbon</u> in the reactivity series have to be extracted using <u>electrolysis</u>, which is expensive.

b) Metals <u>below carbon</u> in the reactivity series can be extracted by <u>reduction</u> using <u>carbon</u>. For example, <u>iron oxide</u> is reduced in a <u>blast furnace</u> to make <u>iron</u>.

This is because carbon <u>can only take the oxygen</u> away from metals which are <u>less reactive</u> than carbon <u>itself</u> is.

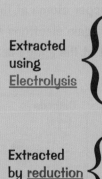

Extracted using **Electrolysis**

Extracted by **reduction** using **carbon**

The Reactivity Series

Potassium	**K**	*more*
Sodium	**Na**	*reactive*
Calcium	**Ca**	
Magnesium	**Mg**	
Aluminium	**Al**	
<u>**CARBON**</u>	<u>**C**</u>	
Zinc	**Zn**	
Iron	**Fe**	
Tin	**Sn**	*less*
Copper	**Cu**	*reactive*

Learn how metals are extracted — ore else...

Extracting metals isn't cheap. You have to pay for special equipment, energy and labour. Then there's the cost of getting the ore to the extraction plant. If there's a choice of extraction methods, a company always picks the <u>cheapest</u>, unless there's a good reason not to (e.g. to increase purity). They're <u>not</u> extracting it for fun.

Getting Metals from Rocks

You may think you know all you could ever want to know about how to get metals from rocks, but no — there's <u>more</u> of it. Think of each of the facts on this page as a little <u>gold nugget</u>. Or, er, a copper one.

Some Metals *have to be* Extracted *by* Electrolysis

1) Metals that are <u>more reactive</u> than carbon (see previous page) have to be extracted using electrolysis of <u>molten compounds</u>.

2) An example of a metal that has to be extracted this way is <u>aluminium</u>.

3) However, the process is <u>much more expensive</u> than reduction with carbon (see previous page) because it <u>uses a lot of energy</u>.

> <u>FOR EXAMPLE</u>: a <u>high temperature</u> is needed to <u>melt</u> aluminium oxide so that <u>aluminium</u> can be extracted — this requires a lot of <u>energy</u>, which makes it an <u>expensive</u> process.

Copper *is* Purified *by* Electrolysis

1) Copper can be easily extracted by <u>reduction with carbon</u> (see previous page). The ore is <u>heated</u> in a <u>furnace</u> — this is called <u>smelting</u>.

2) However, the copper produced this way is <u>impure</u> — and impure copper <u>doesn't</u> conduct electricity very well. This <u>isn't</u> very <u>useful</u> because a lot of copper is used to make <u>electrical wiring</u>.

3) So <u>electrolysis</u> is also used to <u>purify</u> it, even though it's quite <u>expensive</u>.

4) This produces <u>very pure</u> copper, which is a <u>much better conductor</u>.

> You could <u>extract</u> copper straight from its ore by electrolysis if you wanted to, but it's more expensive than using reduction with carbon.

Electrolysis Means "Splitting Up with Electricity"

1) <u>Electrolysis</u> is the <u>breaking down</u> of a substance using <u>electricity</u>.

2) It requires a <u>liquid</u> to <u>conduct</u> the <u>electricity</u>, called the <u>electrolyte</u>.

3) Electrolytes are often <u>metal salt solutions</u> made from the ore (e.g. copper sulfate) or <u>molten metal oxides</u>.

4) The electrolyte has <u>free ions</u> — these <u>conduct</u> the electricity and allow the whole thing to work.

5) Electrons are <u>taken away</u> by the <u>(positive) anode</u> and <u>given away</u> by the <u>(negative) cathode</u>. As ions gain or lose electrons they become atoms or molecules and are released.

> Here's how electrolysis is used to get <u>copper</u>:
> 1) <u>Electrons</u> are <u>pulled off</u> copper atoms at the <u>anode</u>, causing them to go into solution as Cu^{2+} <u>ions</u>.
> 2) Cu^{2+} <u>ions</u> near the <u>cathode</u> gain electrons and turn back into <u>copper atoms</u>.
> 3) The <u>impurities</u> are dropped at the <u>anode</u> as a <u>sludge</u>, whilst <u>pure copper atoms</u> bond to the <u>cathode</u>.

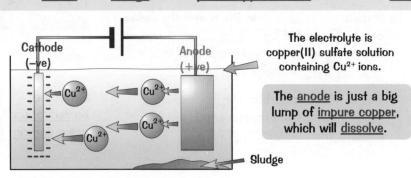

The cathode starts as a <u>thin</u> piece of <u>pure copper</u> and more pure copper <u>adds</u> to it.

Cathode (−ve)

Anode (+ve)

The electrolyte is copper(II) sulfate solution containing Cu^{2+} ions.

The <u>anode</u> is just a big lump of <u>impure copper</u>, which will <u>dissolve</u>.

Sludge

Someone robbed your metal? — call a copper...

The skin of the <u>Statue of Liberty</u> is made of copper — about 80 tonnes of it in fact. Its surface reacts with gases in the air to form <u>copper carbonate</u> — which is why it's that pretty shade of <u>green</u>.

Getting Metals from Rocks

Just to top it off, you need to know even more about copper extraction... sigh, it's a hard life.

You Can Extract Copper From a Solution Using a Displacement Reaction

1) More reactive metals react more vigorously than less reactive metals.

2) If you put a reactive metal into a solution of a dissolved metal compound, the reactive metal will replace the less reactive metal in the compound.

3) This is because the more reactive metal bonds more strongly to the non-metal bit of the compound and pushes out the less reactive metal.

4) For example, scrap iron can be used to displace copper from solution — this is really useful because iron is cheap but copper is expensive. If some iron is put in a solution of copper sulfate, the more reactive iron will "kick out" the less reactive copper from the solution. You end up with iron sulfate solution and copper metal.

copper sulfate + iron → iron sulfate + copper

5) If a piece of silver metal is put into a solution of copper sulfate, nothing happens. The more reactive metal (copper) is already in the solution.

Copper-rich Ores are in Short Supply

1) The supply of copper-rich ores is limited, so it's important to recycle as much copper as possible.

2) The demand for copper is growing and this may lead to shortages in the future.

3) Scientists are looking into new ways of extracting copper from low-grade ores (ores that only contain small amounts of copper) or from the waste that is currently produced when copper is extracted.

4) Examples of new methods to extract copper are bioleaching and phytomining:

Bioleaching

This uses bacteria to separate copper from copper sulfide. The bacteria get energy from the bond between copper and sulfur, separating out the copper from the ore in the process. The leachate (the solution produced by the process) contains copper, which can be extracted, e.g. by filtering.

Phytomining

This involves growing plants in soil that contains copper.
The plants can't use or get rid of the copper so it gradually builds up in the leaves. The plants can be harvested, dried and burned in a furnace.
The copper can be collected from the ash left in the furnace.

5) Traditional methods of copper mining are pretty damaging to the environment (see next page). These new methods of extraction have a much smaller impact, but the disadvantage is that they're slow.

Personally, I'd rather be pound rich than copper rich...

Pure copper is expensive but exceptionally useful stuff. Just think where we'd be without good quality copper wire to conduct electricity (hmmm... how would I live without my electric pineapple corer). The fact that copper-rich ore supplies are dwindling means that scientists have to come up with ever-more-cunning methods to extract it. It also means that you have to learn all about it. Sorry about that.

Impacts of Extracting Metals

Metals are very useful. Just imagine if all knives and forks were made of plastic instead — there'd be prongs snapping all over the place at dinner time. However, metal extraction uses a lot of <u>energy</u> and is <u>bad</u> for the <u>environment</u>. And that's where recycling comes in handy.

Metal Extraction <u>can be</u> Bad <u>for the</u> Environment

1) People have to balance the <u>social</u>, <u>economic</u> and <u>environmental</u> effects of mining the ores.

2) Most of the issues are exactly the same as those to do with quarrying limestone on page 18.

So mining metal ores is <u>good</u> because it means that <u>useful products</u> can be made. It also provides local people with <u>jobs</u> and brings <u>money</u> into the area. This means services such as <u>transport</u> and <u>health</u> can be improved.

But mining ores is <u>bad for the environment</u> as it causes noise, scarring of the landscape and loss of habitats. Deep mine shafts can also be <u>dangerous</u> for a long time after the mine has been abandoned.

Recycling <u>Metals is</u> Important

1) Mining and extracting metals takes lots of <u>energy</u>, most of which comes from burning <u>fossil fuels</u>.

2) Fossil fuels are <u>running out</u> so it's important to <u>conserve</u> them. Not only this, but burning them contributes to <u>acid rain</u>, <u>global dimming</u> and <u>climate change</u> (see pages 28 and 29).

3) Recycling metals only uses a <u>small fraction</u> of the energy needed to mine and extract new metal. E.g. recycling copper only takes 15% of the energy that's needed to mine and extract new copper.

4) Energy doesn't come cheap, so recycling <u>saves money</u> too.

5) Also, there's a <u>finite amount</u> of each <u>metal</u> in the Earth. Recycling conserves these resources.

6) Recycling metal cuts down on the amount of rubbish that gets sent to <u>landfill</u>. Landfill takes up space and <u>pollutes</u> the surroundings. If all the aluminium cans in the UK were recycled, there'd be 14 million fewer dustbins to empty each year.

Get back on your bike again — recycle...

Recycling metals saves <u>natural resources</u> and <u>money</u> and reduces <u>environmental problems</u>. It's great. There's no limit to the number of times metals like aluminium, copper and steel can be recycled. So your humble little drink can may one day form part of a powerful robot who takes over the galaxy.

Properties of Metals

Metals are all the same but slightly different. They have some basic properties in common, but each has its own specific combination of properties, which mean you use different ones for different purposes.

Metals are Strong and Bendy and They're Great Conductors

1) Most of the elements are metals — so they cover most of the periodic table.
   In fact, only the elements on the far right are non-metals.

2) All metals have some fairly similar basic properties:

   - Metals are strong (hard to break), but they can be bent or hammered into different shapes.
   - They're great at conducting heat.
   - They conduct electricity well.

The coloured elements are metals
Just look at 'em all
— there's loads of 'em!

Transition Metals

3) Metals (and especially transition metals, which are found in the centre block of the periodic table) have loads of everyday uses because of these properties...

   - Their strength and 'bendability' makes them handy for making into things like bridges and car bodies.
   - Metals are ideal if you want to make something that heat needs to travel through, like a saucepan base.
   - And their conductivity makes them great for making things like electrical wires.

A Metal's Exact Properties Decide How It's Best Used

1) The properties above are typical properties of metals.
   Not all metals are the same though — you need to learn the specific properties of these three metals:

   Copper is a good conductor of electricity, so it's ideal for drawing out into electrical wires. It's hard and strong but can be bent. It also doesn't react with water.

   Aluminium is corrosion-resistant and has a low density. Pure aluminium isn't particularly strong, but it forms hard, strong alloys (see page 24).

   Titanium is another low density metal. Unlike aluminium it's very strong. It is also corrosion-resistant.

2) Different metals are chosen for different uses because of their specific properties. For example:

   - If you were doing some plumbing, you'd pick a metal that could be bent to make pipes and tanks, and is below hydrogen in the reactivity series so it doesn't react with water. Copper is great for this.
   - If you wanted to make an aeroplane, you'd probably use metal as it's strong and can be bent into shape. But you'd also need it to be light, so aluminium would be a good choice.
   - And if you were making replacement hips, you'd pick a metal that won't corrode when it comes in contact with water. It'd also have to be light too, and not too bendy. Titanium has all of these properties so it's used for this.

Metals are Good — but Not Perfect

1) Metals are very useful structural materials, but some corrode when exposed to air and water, so they need to be protected, e.g. by painting. If metals corrode, they lose their strength and hardness.

2) Metals can get 'tired' when stresses and strains are repeatedly put on them over time. This is known as metal fatigue and leads to metals breaking, which can be very dangerous, e.g. in planes.

Metal fatigue? — yeah, I've had enough of this page too...

So, all metals conduct electricity and heat and can be bent into shape. But lots of them have special properties too. You have to decide what properties you need and use the metal with those properties.

Alloys

Pure metals often aren't quite right for certain jobs. Scientists don't just make do, oh no my friend... they <u>mix two metals together</u> (or mix a metal with a non-metal) — creating an <u>alloy</u> with the properties they want.

Pure Iron **Tends to be a** _Bit Too Bendy_

1) 'Iron' straight from the blast furnace is only <u>96% iron</u>. The other 4% is impurities such as <u>carbon</u>.

2) This impure iron is used as <u>cast iron</u>. It's handy for making <u>ornamental railings</u>, but it doesn't have many other uses because it's <u>brittle</u>.

3) So <u>all</u> the impurities are removed from most of the blast furnace iron. This pure iron has a <u>regular arrangement</u> of identical atoms. The layers of atoms can <u>slide over each other</u>, which makes the iron <u>soft</u> and <u>easily shaped</u>. This iron is far <u>too bendy</u> for most uses.

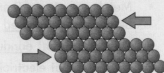

Most Iron is Converted into _Steel_ **— an** _Alloy_

Most of the pure iron is changed into <u>alloys</u> called <u>steels</u>. Steels are formed by adding <u>small</u> amounts of <u>carbon</u> and sometimes <u>other metals</u> to the iron.

TYPE OF STEEL	PROPERTIES	USES
Low carbon steel (0.1% carbon)	easily shaped	car bodies
High carbon steel (1.5% carbon)	very hard, inflexible	blades for cutting tools, bridges
Stainless steel (chromium added, and sometimes nickel)	corrosion-resistant	cutlery, containers for corrosive substances

Alloys **are Harder** _Than_ Pure Metals

1) Different elements have <u>different sized atoms</u>. So when an element such as carbon is added to pure iron, the <u>smaller</u> carbon atom will <u>upset</u> the layers of pure iron atoms, making it more difficult for them to slide over each other. So alloys are <u>harder</u>.

2) Many metals in use today are actually <u>alloys</u>. E.g.:

BRONZE = COPPER + TIN Bronze is <u>harder</u> than copper. It's good for making medals and statues from.

CUPRONICKEL = COPPER + NICKEL This is <u>hard</u> and <u>corrosion resistant</u>. It's used to make "silver" coins.

GOLD ALLOYS ARE USED TO MAKE JEWELLERY Pure gold is <u>too soft</u>. Metals such as zinc, copper, silver, palladium and nickel are used to harden the "gold".

ALUMINIUM ALLOYS ARE USED TO MAKE AIRCRAFT Aluminium has a <u>low density</u>, but it's <u>alloyed</u> with small amounts of other metals to make it <u>stronger</u>.

3) In the past, the development of alloys was by <u>trial and error</u>. But nowadays we understand much more about the properties of metals, so alloys can be <u>designed</u> for specific uses.

A brass band — harder than Iron Maiden...

The <u>Eiffel Tower</u> is made of iron — but the problem with iron is, it goes <u>rusty</u> if air and water get to it. So the Eiffel Tower has to be <u>painted</u> every seven years to make sure that it doesn't rust. This is quite a job and takes an entire year for a team of 25 painters. Too bad they didn't use stainless steel.

Fractional Distillation of Crude Oil

Crude oil is formed from the buried remains of plants and animals — it's a fossil fuel. Over millions of years, the remains turn to crude oil, which can be extracted by drilling and pumping.

Crude Oil is a Mixture of Hydrocarbons

1) A mixture consists of two (or more) elements or compounds that aren't chemically bonded to each other.

2) Crude oil is a mixture of many different compounds. Most of the compounds are hydrocarbon molecules.

3) Hydrocarbons are basically fuels such as petrol and diesel. They're made of just carbon and hydrogen.

4) There are no chemical bonds between the different parts of a mixture, so the different hydrocarbon molecules in crude oil aren't chemically bonded to one another.

5) This means that they all keep their original properties, such as their condensing points. The properties of a mixture are just a mixture of the properties of the separate parts.

6) The parts of a mixture can be separated out by physical methods, e.g. crude oil can be split up into its separate fractions by fractional distillation. Each fraction contains molecules with a similar number of carbon atoms to each other (see next page).

Crude Oil is Split into Separate Groups of Hydrocarbons

The fractionating column works continuously, with heated crude oil piped in at the bottom. The vaporised oil rises up the column and the various fractions are constantly tapped off at the different levels where they condense.

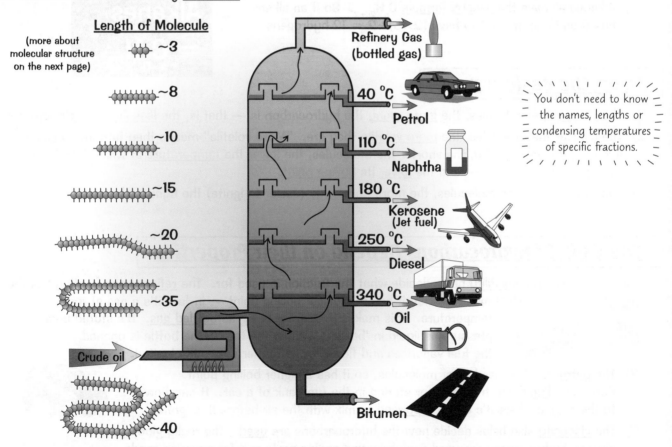

Length of Molecule

(more about molecular structure on the next page)

~3
~8
~10
~15
~20
~35
~40

Refinery Gas (bottled gas)

40 °C — Petrol

110 °C — Naphtha

180 °C — Kerosene (Jet fuel)

250 °C — Diesel

340 °C — Oil

Crude oil

Bitumen

You don't need to know the names, lengths or condensing temperatures of specific fractions.

Crude oil — it's always cracking dirty jokes...

It's amazing what you get from buried dead stuff. But it has had a few hundred million years with high temperature and pressure to get into the useful state it's in now. So if we use it all, we're going to have to wait an awful long time for more to form. No one knows exactly when oil will run out, but some scientists reckon that it could be within this century. The thing is, technology is advancing all the time, so one day it's likely that we'll be able to extract oil that's too difficult and expensive to extract at the moment.

Properties and Uses of Crude Oil

The different fractions of crude oil have different properties, and it's all down to their structure. You need to know the basic structure and a few trends, so you can apply what you've learnt to exam questions.

Crude Oil is Mostly Alkanes

1) All the fractions of crude oil are hydrocarbons called alkanes.
2) Alkanes are made up of chains of carbon atoms surrounded by hydrogen atoms.
3) Different alkanes have chains of different lengths.
4) The first four alkanes are methane (natural gas), ethane, propane and butane.

1) Methane
Formula: CH_4

2) Ethane
Formula: C_2H_6

3) Propane
Formula: C_3H_8

4) Butane
Formula: C_4H_{10}

Each straight line shows a covalent bond (page 15).

5) Carbon atoms form four bonds and hydrogen atoms only form one bond. The diagrams above show that all the atoms have formed bonds with as many other atoms as they can — this means they're saturated.

6) Alkanes all have the general formula C_nH_{2n+2}. So if an alkane has 5 carbons, it's got to have $(2\times5)+2 = 12$ hydrogens.

Alkanes = C_nH_{2n+2}

Learn the Basic Trends:

1) The shorter the molecules, the more runny the hydrocarbon is — that is, the less viscous (gloopy) it is.

2) The shorter the molecules, the more volatile they are. "More volatile" means they turn into a gas at a lower temperature. So, the shorter the molecules, the lower the temperature at which that fraction vaporises or condenses — and the lower its boiling point.

3) Also, the shorter the molecules, the more flammable (easier to ignite) the hydrocarbon is.

The Uses Of Hydrocarbons Depend on their Properties

1) The volatility helps decide what the fraction is used for. The refinery gas fraction has the shortest molecules, so it has the lowest boiling point — in fact it's a gas at room temperature. This makes it ideal for using as bottled gas. It's stored under pressure as liquid in 'bottles'. When the tap on the bottle is opened, the fuel vaporises and flows to the burner where it's ignited.

2) The petrol fraction has longer molecules, so it has a higher boiling point. Petrol is a liquid which is ideal for storing in the fuel tank of a car. It can flow to the engine where it's easily vaporised to mix with the air before it is ignited.

3) The viscosity also helps decide how the hydrocarbons are used. The really gloopy, viscous hydrocarbons are used for lubricating engine parts and for covering roads.

Alkane ya if you don't learn this...

So short-chain hydrocarbons are less viscous, more volatile and easier to ignite than longer-chain hydrocarbons. If you learn the properties of short-chain hydrocarbons, you should be able to work out the properties of longer-chain ones in the exam. These properties decide how they're used. In the real world there's more demand for stuff like petrol than there is for long gloopy hydrocarbons like bitumen — I guess there's only so many roads that need covering.

Using Crude Oil as a Fuel

Nothing as amazingly useful as crude oil would be without its problems. No, that'd be too good to be true.

Crude Oil Provides an Important Fuel for Modern Life

1) Crude oil fractions burn cleanly so they make good <u>fuels</u>. Most modern transport is fuelled by a crude oil fraction, e.g. cars, boats, trains and planes. Parts of crude oil are also burned in <u>central heating systems</u> in homes and in <u>power stations</u> to <u>generate electricity</u>.

2) There's a <u>massive industry</u> with scientists working to find oil reserves, take it out of the ground, and turn it into useful products. As well as fuels, crude oil also provides the raw materials for making various <u>chemicals</u>, including <u>plastics</u>.

3) Often, <u>alternatives</u> to using crude oil fractions as fuel are possible. E.g. electricity can be generated by <u>nuclear</u> power or <u>wind</u> power, there are <u>ethanol</u>-powered cars, and <u>solar</u> energy can be used to heat water.

4) But things tend to be <u>set up</u> for using oil fractions. For example, cars are designed for <u>petrol or diesel</u> and it's <u>readily available</u>. There are filling stations all over the country, with storage facilities and pumps specifically designed for these crude oil fractions. So crude oil fractions are often the <u>easiest and cheapest</u> thing to use.

5) Crude oil fractions are often <u>more reliable</u> too — e.g. solar and wind power won't work without the right weather conditions. Nuclear energy is reliable, but there are lots of concerns about its <u>safety</u> and the storage of radioactive waste.

But it Might Run Out One Day... Eeek

1) Most scientists think that oil will <u>run out</u> — it's a <u>non-renewable fuel</u>.

2) No one knows exactly when it'll run out but there have been heaps of <u>different predictions</u> — e.g. about 40 years ago, scientists predicted that it'd all be gone by the year 2000.

3) <u>New oil reserves</u> are discovered from time to time and <u>technology</u> is constantly improving, so it's now possible to extract oil that was once too <u>difficult</u> or <u>expensive</u> to extract.

4) In the <u>worst-case scenario</u>, oil may be pretty much gone in about 25 years — and that's not far off.

5) Some people think we should <u>immediately stop</u> using oil for things like transport, for which there are alternatives, and keep it for things that it's absolutely <u>essential</u> for, like some chemicals and medicines.

6) It will take time to <u>develop</u> alternative fuels that will satisfy all our energy needs (see page 29 for more info). It'll also take time to <u>adapt things</u> so that the fuels can be used on a wide scale. E.g. we might need different kinds of car engines, or special storage tanks built.

7) One alternative is to generate energy from <u>renewable</u> sources — these are sources that <u>won't run out</u>. Examples of renewable energy sources are <u>wind power</u>, <u>solar power</u> and <u>tidal power</u>.

8) So however long oil does last for, it's a good idea to start <u>conserving</u> it and finding <u>alternatives</u> now.

Crude Oil is NOT the Environment's Best Friend

1) <u>Oil spills</u> can happen as the oil is being transported by tanker — this spells <u>disaster</u> for the local environment. <u>Birds</u> get covered in the stuff and are <u>poisoned</u> as they try to clean themselves. Other creatures, like <u>sea otters</u> and <u>whales</u>, are poisoned too.

2) You have to <u>burn oil</u> to release the energy from it. But burning oil is thought to be a major cause of <u>global warming</u>, <u>acid rain</u> and <u>global dimming</u> — see pages 28 and 29.

If oil alternatives aren't developed, we might get caught short...

Crude oil is <u>really important</u> to our lives. Take <u>petrol</u> for instance — at the first whisper of a shortage, there's mayhem. Loads of people dash to the petrol station and start filling up their tanks. This causes a queue, which starts everyone else panicking. I don't know what they'll do when it runs out totally.

Environmental Problems

We burn fuels all the time to release the energy stored inside them — e.g. 90% of crude oil is used as fuel.

Burning Fossil Fuels *Releases* Gases *and* Particles

1) Power stations burn huge amounts of fossil fuels to make electricity. Cars are also a major culprit in burning fossil fuels.

2) Most fuels, such as crude oil and coal, contain carbon and hydrogen. During combustion, the carbon and hydrogen are oxidised so that carbon dioxide and water vapour are released into the atmosphere. Energy (heat) is also produced.

E.g.:

> hydrocarbon + oxygen → carbon dioxide + water vapour

Pure hydrogen can also be used as a fuel (see next page). It only produces water vapour when burnt.

3) If the fuel contains sulfur impurities, the sulfur will be released as sulfur dioxide when the fuel is burnt.

4) Oxides of nitrogen will also form if the fuel burns at a high temperature.

5) When there's plenty of oxygen, all the fuel burns — this is called complete combustion.

6) If there's not enough oxygen, some of the fuel doesn't burn — this is called partial combustion. Under these conditions, solid particles (called particulates) of soot (carbon) and unburnt fuel are released. Carbon monoxide (a poisonous gas) is also released.

Sulfur Dioxide *Causes* Acid Rain

1) Sulfur dioxide is one of the gases that causes acid rain.

2) When the sulfur dioxide mixes with clouds it forms dilute sulfuric acid. This then falls as acid rain.

3) In the same way, oxides of nitrogen cause acid rain by forming dilute nitric acid in clouds.

4) Acid rain causes lakes to become acidic and many plants and animals die as a result.

5) Acid rain kills trees and damages limestone buildings and ruins stone statues. It's shocking.

6) Links between acid rain and human health problems have been suggested.

7) The benefits of electricity and travel have to be balanced against the environmental impacts. Governments have recognised the importance of this and international agreements have been put in place to reduce emissions of air pollutants such as sulfur dioxide.

You can Reduce Acid Rain *by* Reducing Sulfur Emissions

1) Most of the sulfur can be removed from fuels before they're burnt, but it costs more to do it.

2) Also, removing sulfur from fuels takes more energy. This usually comes from burning more fuel, which releases more of the greenhouse gas carbon dioxide.

3) However, petrol and diesel are starting to be replaced by low-sulfur versions.

4) Power stations now have Acid Gas Scrubbers to take the harmful gases out before they release their fumes into the atmosphere.

5) The other way of reducing acid rain is simply to reduce our usage of fossil fuels.

Eee, problems, problems — there's always summat goin' wrong...

Pollutants like sulfur dioxide can be carried a long way in the atmosphere. So a country might suffer from acid rain that it didn't cause, which doesn't seem very fair. It's not just up to big industries though — there's lots of things you can do to reduce the amount of fossil fuels burnt. Putting an extra jumper on instead of turning up the heating helps. As does walking places instead of cadging a lift.

More Environmental Problems

More doom and gloom on this page I'm afraid... You've got to know it all though.

Increasing Carbon Dioxide **Causes** Climate Change

1) The level of carbon dioxide in the atmosphere is increasing — because of the large amounts of fossil fuels humans burn.

2) There's a scientific consensus that this extra carbon dioxide has caused the average temperature of the Earth to increase — global warming.

3) Global warming is a type of climate change and causes other types of climate change, e.g. changing rainfall patterns. It could also cause severe flooding due to the polar ice caps melting.

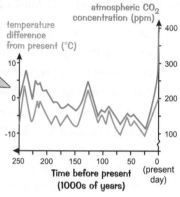

Particles **Cause** Global Dimming

1) In the last few years, some scientists have been measuring how much sunlight is reaching the surface of the Earth and comparing it to records from the last 50 years.

2) They have been amazed to find that in some areas nearly 25% less sunlight has been reaching the surface compared to 50 years ago. They have called this global dimming.

3) They think that it is caused by particles of soot and ash that are produced when fossil fuels are burnt. These particles reflect sunlight back into space, or they can help to produce more clouds that reflect the sunlight back into space.

4) There are many scientists who don't believe the change is real and blame it on inaccurate recording equipment.

Alternative Fuels **are Being Developed**

Some alternative fuels have already been developed, and there are others in the pipeline (so to speak). Many of them are renewable fuels so, unlike fossil fuels, they won't run out. However, none of them are perfect — they all have pros and cons. For example:

ETHANOL can be produced from plant material so is known as a biofuel. It's made by fermentation of plants and is used to power cars in some places. It's often mixed with petrol to make a better fuel.

PROS: The CO_2 released when it's burnt was taken in by the plant as it grew, so it's 'carbon neutral'. The only other product is water.

CONS: Engines need to be converted before they'll work with ethanol fuels. And ethanol fuel isn't widely available. There are worries that as demand for it increases farmers will switch from growing food crops to growing crops to make ethanol — this will increase food prices.

BIODIESEL is another type of biofuel. It can be produced from vegetable oils such as rapeseed oil and soybean oil. Biodiesel can be mixed with ordinary diesel fuel and used to run a diesel engine.

PROS: Biodiesel is 'carbon neutral'. Engines don't need to be converted. It produces much less sulfur dioxide and 'particulates' than ordinary diesel or petrol.

CONS: We can't make enough to completely replace diesel. It's expensive to make. It could increase food prices like using more ethanol could (see above).

HYDROGEN GAS can also be used to power vehicles. You get the hydrogen from the electrolysis of water — there's plenty of water about but it takes electrical energy to split it up. This energy can come from a renewable source, e.g. solar.

PROS: Hydrogen combines with oxygen in the air to form just water — so it's very clean.

CONS: You need a special, expensive engine and hydrogen isn't widely available. You still need to use energy from another source to make it. Also, hydrogen's hard to store.

Global dimming — romantic lighting all day...

Alternative fuels are the shining light at the end of a long tunnel of problems caused by burning fuels (and I mean long). But nothing's perfect (except my quiff... and maybe my golf swing), so get learnin' those disadvantages.

Revision Summary for Chemistry 1a

There wasn't anything too ghastly in this section, and a few bits were even quite interesting I reckon. But you've got to make sure the facts are all firmly embedded in your brain and that you really understand the issues. These questions will let you see what you know and what you don't. If you get stuck on any, you need to look at that stuff again. Keep going till you can do them all without coming up for air.

1) Sketch an atom. Label the nucleus and the electrons.

2) What are the symbols for: a) calcium, b) carbon, c) sodium?

3)* Which element's properties are more similar to magnesium's: calcium or iron?

4) Describe how you would work out the electronic structure of an atom given its atomic number.

5) Describe the process of ionic bonding.

6) What is covalent bonding?

7)* Say which of the diagrams on the right show:
   a) an element   and   b) a compound
   Suggest what elements or compounds could be in each.

8)* Balance these equations:
   a) $CaCO_3 + HCl \rightarrow CaCl_2 + H_2O + CO_2$ b) $Ca + H_2O \rightarrow Ca(OH)_2 + H_2$

9) Write down the symbol equation showing the thermal decomposition of limestone.

10) What products are produced when limestone reacts with an acid?

11) What is calcium hydroxide used for?

12) Name three building materials made from limestone.

13) Plans to develop a limestone quarry and a cement factory on some hills next to your town are announced. Describe the views that the following might have:
    a) dog owners   b) a mother of young children
    c) the owner of a cafe   d) a beetle

14) What's the definition of an ore?

15) Explain why zinc can be extracted by reduction with carbon but magnesium can't.

16) Give a reason why aluminium is an expensive metal.

17) What is electrolysis?

18) Describe the process of purifying copper by electrolysis.

19) Describe how scrap iron is used to displace copper from solution.

20) What is the name of the method where plants are used to extract metals from soil?

21) Give three reasons why it's good to recycle metal.

22) Give three properties of metals.

23) Briefly describe two problems with metals.

24) What is the problem with using a) iron straight from the blast furnace, b) very pure iron?

25) Give two examples of alloys and say what's in them.

26) What does crude oil consist of? What does fractional distillation do to crude oil?

27) What's the general formula for an alkane?

28) Is a short-chain hydrocarbon more viscous than a long-chain hydrocarbon? Is it more volatile?

29)* You're going on holiday to a very cold place. The temperature will be about −10 °C. Which of the fuels shown on the right do you think will work best in your camping stove? Explain your answer.

Fuel	Boiling point (°C)
Propane	−42
Butane	−0.4
Pentane	36.2

30) Name three pollutants released into the atmosphere when fuels are burned. What environmental problems are associated with each?

31) List three ways of reducing acid rain.

32) Has the theory of global dimming been proven?

33) List three alternative ways of powering cars. What are the pros and cons of each?

* Answers on page 100.

Cracking Crude Oil

After the distillation of crude oil (see page 25), you've still got both short and long hydrocarbons, just not all mixed together. But there's <u>more demand</u> for some products, like <u>petrol</u>, than for others.

Cracking Means Splitting Up Long–chain Hydrocarbons...

1) <u>Long-chain hydrocarbons</u> form <u>thick gloopy liquids</u> like <u>tar</u> which aren't all that useful, so...

2) ... a lot of the longer molecules produced from <u>fractional distillation</u> are <u>turned into smaller ones</u> by a process called <u>cracking</u>.

3) Some of the products of cracking are useful as fuels, e.g. petrol for cars and paraffin for jet fuel.

4) Cracking also produces substances like <u>ethene</u>, which are needed for <u>making plastics</u> (see page 33).

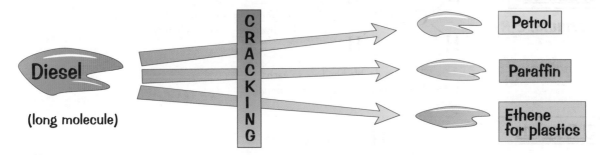

Diesel (long molecule) → CRACKING → Petrol, Paraffin, Ethene for plastics

...by Passing Vapour Over a Hot Catalyst

1) <u>Cracking</u> is a <u>thermal decomposition</u> reaction — <u>breaking molecules down</u> by <u>heating</u> them.

2) The first step is to <u>heat</u> the long-chain hydrocarbon to <u>vaporise</u> it (turn it into a gas).

3) Then the <u>vapour</u> is passed over a <u>powdered catalyst</u> at a temperature of about <u>400 °C – 700 °C</u>.

4) <u>Aluminium oxide</u> is the catalyst used.

5) The <u>long-chain</u> molecules <u>split apart</u> or "crack" on the <u>surface</u> of the specks of catalyst.

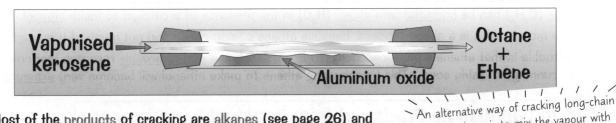

Vaporised kerosene → Octane + Ethene. Aluminium oxide

6) Most of the <u>products</u> of cracking are <u>alkanes</u> (see page 26) and unsaturated hydrocarbons called <u>alkenes</u> (see page 32)...

An alternative way of cracking long-chain hydrocarbons is to mix the vapour with steam at a very high temperature.

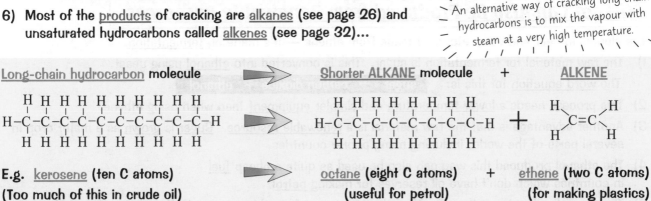

Long-chain hydrocarbon molecule ⟹ Shorter ALKANE molecule + ALKENE

E.g. <u>kerosene</u> (ten C atoms) ⟹ <u>octane</u> (eight C atoms) + <u>ethene</u> (two C atoms)
(Too much of this in crude oil)   (useful for petrol)   (for making plastics)

Get cracking — there's a lot to learn...

Crude oil is <u>useful stuff</u>, there's no doubt about it. But using it is not without its problems (see page 27 for more about fuels). For example, oil is shipped around the planet, which can lead to <u>slicks</u> if there's an accident. Also, burning oil is thought to cause <u>climate change</u>, <u>acid rain</u> and <u>global dimming</u>. Oil is going to start <u>running out</u> one day, which will lead to big difficulties.

Alkenes and Ethanol

Alkenes are very useful. You can use them to make all sorts of stuff.

Alkenes Have a C=C Double Bond

1) Alkenes are hydrocarbons which have a <u>double bond</u> between two of the <u>carbon</u> atoms in their chain.

2) They are known as <u>unsaturated</u> because they <u>can make more bonds</u> — the double bond can open up, allowing the two carbon atoms to bond with other atoms.

3) The first two alkenes are <u>ethene</u> (with two carbon atoms) and <u>propene</u> (three Cs).

4) <u>All alkenes</u> have the general formula: C_nH_{2n} — they have twice as many hydrogens as carbons.

1) Ethene

Formula: C_2H_4

Carbon atoms always make four bonds, but hydrogen atoms only make one.

This is a double bond — so each carbon atom is still making four bonds.

2) Propene

Formula: C_3H_6

bromine water + alkene — decolourised

5) You can test for an alkene by adding the substance to <u>bromine water</u>. An alkene will <u>decolourise</u> the bromine water, turning it from <u>orange</u> to <u>colourless</u>. This is because the <u>double bond</u> has <u>opened</u> up and formed bonds with the bromine.

Ethene Can Be Reacted with Steam to Produce Ethanol

1) <u>Ethene</u> (C_2H_4) can be <u>hydrated</u> with <u>steam</u> (H_2O) in the presence of a catalyst to make <u>ethanol</u>.

2) At the moment this is a <u>cheap</u> process, because ethene's fairly <u>cheap</u> and <u>not much</u> of it is <u>wasted</u>.

3) The trouble is that ethene's produced from crude oil, which is a <u>non-renewable</u> resource that could start running out fairly soon. This means using ethene to make ethanol will become very <u>expensive</u>.

Ethanol Can Also Be Produced from Renewable Resources

The alcohol in beer and wine, etc. isn't made from ethene — it's made by <u>fermentation</u>.

1) The raw material for fermentation is <u>sugar</u>. This is converted into <u>ethanol</u> using yeast.
   The <u>word equation</u> for this is: sugar   →   carbon dioxide + ethanol

2) This process needs a <u>lower temperature</u> and <u>simpler equipment</u> than when using ethene.

3) Another advantage is that the raw material is a <u>renewable resource</u>. <u>Sugar</u> is <u>grown</u> as a major crop in several parts of the world, including many poorer countries.

4) The ethanol produced this way can also be used as quite a cheap <u>fuel</u> in countries which don't have oil reserves for making <u>petrol</u>.

5) There are <u>disadvantages</u> though. The ethanol you get from this process <u>isn't very concentrated</u>, so if you want to increase its strength you have to <u>distil</u> it (as in whisky distilleries). It also needs to be <u>purified</u>.

Make ethanol — not war...

Don't get alk<u>e</u>nes confused with alk<u>a</u>nes — that one letter makes all the difference. Alkenes have a C=C bond, alkanes don't. The first parts of their names are the same though — "eth-" means "<u>two</u> C atoms", "prop-" means "<u>three</u> C atoms". And remember — alkenes decolourise <u>bromine water</u> and alkanes don't.

Using Alkenes to Make Polymers

Before we knew how to make polymers, there were no polythene bags. Everyone used string bags for their shopping. Now we have plastic bags that hurt your hands and split halfway home.

Alkenes Can Be Used to Make Polymers

1) Probably the most useful thing you can do with alkenes is polymerisation. This means joining together lots of small alkene molecules (monomers) to form very large molecules — these long-chain molecules are called polymers.

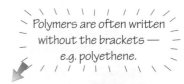
Polymers are often written without the brackets — e.g. polyethene.

2) For instance, many ethene molecules can be joined up to produce poly(ethene) or "polythene".

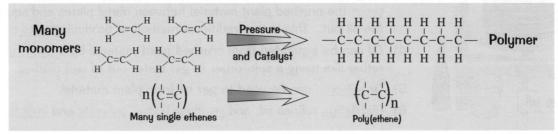

3) In the same way, if you join lots of propene molecules together, you've got poly(propene).

Different Polymers Have Different Physical Properties...

1) The physical properties of a polymer depend on what it's made from. Polyamides are usually stronger than poly(ethene), for example.

2) A polymer's physical properties are also affected by the temperature and pressure of polymerisation. Poly(ethene) made at 200 °C and 2000 atmospheres pressure is flexible, and has low density. But poly(ethene) made at 60 °C and a few atmospheres pressure with a catalyst is rigid and dense.

...Which Make Them Suitable for Various Different Uses

1) Light, stretchable polymers such as low density poly(ethene) are used to make plastic bags. Elastic polymer fibres are used to make super-stretchy LYCRA® fibre for tights.

2) New uses are developed all the time. Waterproof coatings for fabrics are made of polymers. Dental polymers are used in resin tooth fillings. Polymer hydrogel wound dressings keep wounds moist.

3) New biodegradable packaging materials made from polymers and cornstarch are being produced.

4) Memory foam is an example of a smart material. It's a polymer that gets softer as it gets warmer. Mattresses can be made of memory foam — they mould to your body shape when you lie on them.

Polymers Are Cheap, but Most Don't Rot — They're Hard to Get Rid Of

1) Most polymers aren't "biodegradable" — they're not broken down by microorganisms, so they don't rot.

2) It's difficult to get rid of them — if you bury them in a landfill site, they'll still be there years later. The best thing is to re-use them as many times as possible and then recycle them if you can.

3) Things made from polymers are usually cheaper than things made from metal. However, as crude oil resources get used up, the price of crude oil will rise. Crude oil products like polymers will get dearer.

4) It may be that one day there won't be enough oil for fuel AND plastics AND all the other uses. Choosing how to use the oil that's left means weighing up advantages and disadvantages on all sides.

Revision's like a polymer — you join lots of little facts up...

Polymers are all over the place — and I don't just mean all those plastic bags stuck in trees. There are naturally occurring polymers, like rubber and silk. That's quite a few clothing options, even without synthetic polymers like polyester and PVC. You've even got polymers on the inside — DNA's a polymer.

Plant Oils

If you squeeze a <u>walnut</u> really hard, out will ooze some <u>walnut oil</u>, which you could use to make <u>walnut mayonnaise</u>. Much better to just buy some oil from the shop though.

We Can Extract Oils from Plants

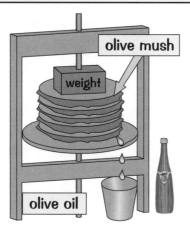

olive mush

weight

olive oil

1) Some <u>fruits</u> and <u>seeds</u> contain a lot of <u>oil</u>. For example, avocados and olives are oily fruits. Brazil nuts, peanuts and sesame seeds are oily seeds (a nut is just a big seed really).

2) These oils can be extracted and used for <u>food</u> or for <u>fuel</u>.

3) To get the oil out, the plant material is <u>crushed</u>. The next step is to <u>press</u> the crushed plant material between metal plates and squash the oil out. This is the traditional method of producing <u>olive oil</u>.

4) Oil can be separated from crushed plant material by a <u>centrifuge</u> — rather like using a spin-dryer to get water out of wet clothes.

5) Or <u>solvents</u> can be used to get oil from plant material.

6) <u>Distillation</u> refines oil, and <u>removes water</u>, <u>solvents</u> and <u>impurities</u>.

Vegetable Oils Are Used in Food

1) Vegetable oils provide a lot of <u>energy</u> — they have a very high energy content.

2) There are other nutrients in vegetable oils. For example, oils from seeds contain <u>vitamin E</u>.

3) Vegetable oils contain <u>essential fatty acids</u>, which the body needs for many metabolic processes.

Vegetable Oils Have Benefits for Cooking

1) Vegetable oils have <u>higher boiling points</u> than water. This means they can be used to cook foods at higher temperatures and at <u>faster</u> speeds.

2) Cooking with vegetable oil gives food a <u>different flavour</u>. This is because of the oil's <u>own</u> flavour, but it's also down to the fact that many flavours come from chemicals that are <u>soluble</u> in oil. This means the oil 'carries' the flavour, making it seem more <u>intense</u>.

3) Using oil to cook food <u>increases</u> the <u>energy</u> we get from eating it.

Vegetable Oils Can Be Used to Produce Fuels

1) Vegetable oils such as rapeseed oil and soybean oil can be <u>processed</u> and turned into <u>fuels</u>.

2) Because vegetable oils provide a lot of <u>energy</u> they're really suitable for use as fuels.

3) A particularly useful fuel made from vegetable oils is called <u>biodiesel</u>. Biodiesel has similar properties to ordinary diesel fuel — it burns in the same way, so you can use it to fuel a diesel engine.

See page 29 for more about biodiesel.

That lippie fried a few sausages back in her heyday...

Plant oils have loads of different uses, from frying bacon to fuelling cars. Even <u>waste oil</u>, left over from manufacturing and cooking in fast food restaurants, ends up being used in <u>pet food</u> and <u>cosmetics</u>. Grim.

Plant Oils

Oils are usually quite runny at room temperature. That's fine for salad dressing, say, but not so good for spreading in your sandwiches. For that, you could hydrogenate the oil to make margarine...

Unsaturated Oils Contain C=C Double Bonds

1) Oils and fats contain long-chain molecules with lots of carbon atoms.
2) Oils and fats are either saturated or unsaturated.
3) Unsaturated oils contain double bonds between some of the carbon atoms in their carbon chains.
4) So, an unsaturated oil will decolourise bromine water (as the bromine opens up the double bond and joins on).
5) Monounsaturated fats contain one C=C double bond somewhere in their carbon chains. Polyunsaturated fats contain more than one C=C double bond.

bromine water + unsaturated oil — decolourised

Unsaturated Oils Can Be Hydrogenated

1) Unsaturated vegetable oils are liquid at room temperature.
2) They can be hardened by reacting them with hydrogen in the presence of a nickel catalyst at about 60 °C. This is called hydrogenation. The hydrogen reacts with the double-bonded carbons and opens out the double bonds.

$$C=C + H_2 \xrightarrow[\text{catalyst}]{\text{nickel}} H-C-C-H$$

3) Hydrogenated oils have higher melting points than unsaturated oils, so they're more solid at room temperature. This makes them useful as spreads and for baking cakes and pastries.
4) Margarine is usually made from partially hydrogenated vegetable oil — turning all the double bonds in vegetable oil to single bonds would make margarine too hard and difficult to spread. Hydrogenating most of them gives margarine a nice, buttery, spreadable consistency.
5) Partially hydrogenated vegetable oils are often used instead of butter in processed foods, e.g. biscuits. These oils are a lot cheaper than butter and they keep longer. This makes biscuits cheaper and gives them a long shelf life.
6) But partially hydrogenating vegetable oils means you end up with a lot of so-called trans fats. And there's evidence to suggest that trans fats are very bad for you.

Vegetable Oils in Foods Can Affect Health

1) Vegetable oils tend to be unsaturated, while animal fats tend to be saturated.
2) In general, saturated fats are less healthy than unsaturated fats (as saturated fats increase the amount of cholesterol in the blood, which can block up the arteries and increase the risk of heart disease).
3) Natural unsaturated fats such as olive oil and sunflower oil reduce the amount of blood cholesterol. But because of the trans fats, partially hydrogenated vegetable oil increases the amount of cholesterol in the blood. So eating a lot of foods made with partially hydrogenated vegetable oils can actually increase the risk of heart disease.
4) Cooking food in oil, whether saturated, unsaturated or partially hydrogenated, makes it more fattening.

Double bonds — licensed to saturate...

This is tricky stuff. In a nutshell... there are saturated and unsaturated fats, which are generally bad and good for you (in that order) — easy enough. But... partially hydrogenated vegetable oil (which is unsaturated) is bad for you. Too much of the wrong types of fats can lead to heart disease. Got that...

Emulsions

Emulsions are all over the place in foods, cosmetics and paint. And in exams...

Emulsions Can Be Made from Oil and Water

1) Oils don't dissolve in water. So far so good...

2) However, you can mix an oil with water to make an emulsion. Emulsions are made up of lots of droplets of one liquid suspended in another liquid. You can have an oil-in-water emulsion (oil droplets suspended in water) or a water-in-oil emulsion (water droplets suspended in oil).

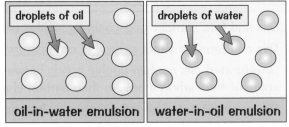

droplets of oil

droplets of water

oil-in-water emulsion | water-in-oil emulsion

3) Emulsions are thicker than either oil or water. E.g. mayonnaise is an emulsion of sunflower oil (or olive oil) and vinegar — it's thicker than either.

4) The physical properties of emulsions make them suited to lots of uses in food — e.g. as salad dressings and in sauces. For instance, a salad dressing made by shaking olive oil and vinegar together forms an emulsion that coats salad better than plain oil or plain vinegar.

5) Generally, the more oil you've got in an oil-in-water emulsion, the thicker it is. Milk is an oil-in-water emulsion with not much oil and a lot of water — there's about 3% oil in full-fat milk. Single cream has a bit more oil — about 18%. Double cream has lots of oil — nearly 50%.

6) Whipped cream and ice cream are oil-in-water emulsions with an extra ingredient — air. Air is whipped into cream to give it a fluffy, frothy consistency for use as a topping. Whipping air into ice cream gives it a softer texture, which makes it easier to scoop out of the tub.

7) Emulsions also have non-food uses. Most moisturising lotions are oil-in-water emulsions. The smooth texture of an emulsion makes it easy to rub into the skin.

Some Foods Contain Emulsifiers to Help Oil and Water Mix

Oil and water mixtures naturally separate out. But here's where emulsifiers come in...

1) Emulsifiers are molecules with one part that's attracted to water and another part that's attracted to oil or fat. The bit that's attracted to water is called hydrophilic, and the bit that's attracted to oil is called hydrophobic.

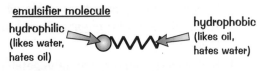

emulsifier molecule

hydrophilic (likes water, hates oil)

hydrophobic (likes oil, hates water)

2) The hydrophilic end of each emulsifier molecule latches onto water molecules.

3) The hydrophobic end of each emulsifier molecule cosies up to oil molecules.

4) When you shake oil and water together with a bit of emulsifier, the oil forms droplets, surrounded by a coating of emulsifier... with the hydrophilic bit facing outwards. Other oil droplets are repelled by the hydrophilic bit of the emulsifier, while water molecules latch on. So the emulsion won't separate out. Clever.

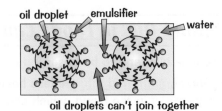

oil droplet | emulsifier | water

oil droplets can't join together

Using Emulsifiers Has Pros and Cons

1) Emulsifiers stop emulsions from separating out and this gives them a longer shelf-life.

2) Emulsifiers allow food companies to produce food that's lower in fat but that still has a good texture.

3) The down side is that some people are allergic to certain emulsifiers. For example, egg yolk is often used as an emulsifier — so people who are allergic to eggs need to check the ingredients very carefully.

Emulsion paint — spread mayonnaise all over the walls...

Before fancy stuff from abroad like olive oil, we fried our bacon and eggs in lard. Mmmm. Lard wouldn't be so good for making salad cream though. Emulsions like salad cream have to be made from shaking up two liquids — tiny droplets of one liquid are 'suspended' (NOT dissolved) in the other liquid.

Plate Tectonics

The Earth's surface is very <u>crinkly</u> — lots of mountains and valleys. Scientists used to think that these 'wrinkles' were caused by the shrinkage of the surface as it cooled down after the Earth was formed. This theory has now been replaced by one that <u>fits the facts</u> better, but most people took a lot of persuading...

Wegener's Theory <u>of</u> Continental Drift...

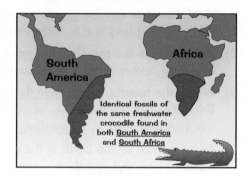

Identical fossils of the same freshwater crocodile found in both <u>South America</u> and <u>South Africa</u>

1) <u>Alfred Wegener</u> came across some work listing the fossils of <u>very similar</u> plants and animals which had been found on <u>opposite sides</u> of the Atlantic Ocean.

2) He investigated further, and found other cases of very similar fossils on opposite sides of oceans.

3) Other people had probably noticed this too. The accepted explanation was that there had once been <u>land bridges</u> linking the continents — so animals had been able to cross. The bridges had 'sunk' or been covered over since then.

4) But Wegener had also noticed that the coastlines of Africa and South America seemed to 'match' like the pieces of a <u>jigsaw</u>. He wondered if these two continents had previously been one continent which then split. He started to look for more evidence, and found it...

5) There were <u>matching layers</u> in the rocks in different continents.

6) Fossils had been found in the 'wrong' places — e.g. fossils of tropical plants had been discovered on Arctic islands, where the present climate would clearly have killed them off.

7) In 1915, Wegener felt he had enough evidence. He published his theory of "<u>continental drift</u>".

8) Wegener said that about 300 million years ago, there had been just one '<u>supercontinent</u>'. This landmass, Pangaea, broke into smaller chunks which moved apart. He claimed that these chunks — our modern-day <u>continents</u> — were still slowly 'drifting' apart.

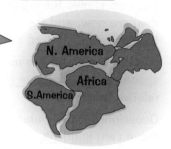

...Wasn't Accepted <u>for</u> Many Years

The reaction from other scientists was mostly very <u>hostile</u>. The main problem was that Wegener's explanation of <u>how</u> the '<u>drifting</u>' happened wasn't very convincing.

1) Wegener thought that the continents were 'ploughing through' the sea bed, and that their movement was caused by tidal forces and the earth's rotation.

2) Other geologists said this was <u>impossible</u>. One scientist calculated that the forces needed to move the continents like this would also have stopped the Earth rotating. (Which it hadn't.)

3) Wegener had used <u>inaccurate data</u> in his calculations, so he'd made some rather <u>wild predictions</u> about how fast the continents ought to be moving apart.

4) A few scientists supported Wegener, but most of them didn't see any reason to believe such a strange theory. It probably didn't help that he wasn't a 'proper' geologist — he'd studied astronomy.

5) Then in the 1950s, scientists were able to investigate the <u>ocean floor</u> and found <u>new evidence</u> to support Wegener's theory. He wasn't right about everything, but his <u>main idea</u> was <u>correct</u>.

6) By the 1960s, geologists were <u>convinced</u>. We now think the Earth's crust is made of several chunks called <u>tectonic plates</u> which move about, and that colliding chunks push the land up to create mountains.

I told you so — but no one ever believes me...

Sadly, Wegener died before his theory was accepted (when hundreds of geologists had to rewrite their textbooks). His story is a classic example of how science progresses — someone puts forward an idea, everyone else points out why it's nonsense, and eventually the really <u>good</u> ideas are accepted.

The Earth's Structure

No one accepted the theory of <u>plate tectonics</u> for ages. Almost everyone does now. How times change.

The <u>Earth</u> Has a <u>Crust</u>, <u>Mantle</u>, <u>Outer</u> and <u>Inner Core</u>

The Earth is <u>almost spherical</u> and it has a <u>layered</u> structure, a bit like a scotch egg. Or a peach.

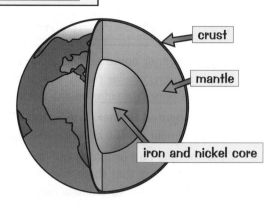

1) The bit we live on, the <u>crust</u>, is very <u>thin</u> (it varies between 5 km and 50 km) and is surrounded by the <u>atmosphere</u>.

2) Below that is the <u>mantle</u>. The <u>mantle</u> has all the properties of a <u>solid</u>, except that it can flow very <u>slowly</u>.

3) Within the mantle, <u>radioactive decay</u> takes place. This produces a lot of <u>heat</u>, which causes the mantle to <u>flow</u> in <u>convection currents</u>.

4) At the centre of the Earth is the <u>core</u>, which we think is made of <u>iron and nickel</u>.

The <u>Earth's Surface</u> is Made Up of <u>Tectonic Plates</u>

1) The crust and the upper part of the mantle are cracked into a number of large pieces called <u>tectonic plates</u>. These plates are a bit like <u>big rafts</u> that 'float' on the mantle.

2) The plates don't stay in one place though. That's because the <u>convection currents</u> in the mantle cause the plates to <u>drift</u>.

3) The map shows the <u>edges</u> of the plates as they are now, and the <u>directions</u> they're moving in (red arrows).

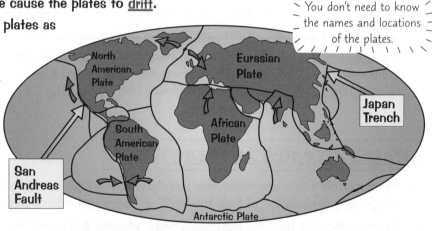

4) Most of the plates are moving at speeds of <u>a few cm per year</u> relative to each other.

5) Occasionally, the plates move very <u>suddenly</u>, causing an <u>earthquake</u>.

6) <u>Volcanoes</u> and <u>earthquakes</u> often occur at the boundaries between two tectonic plates.

Scientists Can't <u>Predict</u> Earthquakes and Volcanic Eruptions

1) Tectonic plates can stay more or less put for a while and then <u>suddenly</u> lurch forwards. It's <u>impossible to predict</u> exactly when they'll move.

2) Scientists are trying to find out if there are any <u>clues</u> that an earthquake might happen soon — things like strain in underground rocks. Even with these clues they'll only be able to say an earthquake's <u>likely</u> to happen, not <u>exactly when</u> it'll happen.

3) There are some <u>clues</u> that say a volcanic eruption might happen soon. Before an eruption, molten rock rises up into chambers near the surface, causing the ground surface to bulge slightly. This causes <u>mini-earthquakes</u> near the volcano.

4) But sometimes molten rock cools down instead of erupting, so mini-earthquakes can be a <u>false alarm</u>.

Plate Tectonics — it's a smashing theory...

There's a mixture of <u>plain facts</u> and <u>scientific thinking</u> here. Learn the details of the Earth's structure, and make sure you can explain how tectonic plates move and what happens at plate boundaries. It's important to remember that earthquakes are unpredictable even with the best equipment.

The Evolution of the Atmosphere

For 200 million years or so, the atmosphere has been about how it is now: 78% nitrogen, 21% oxygen, and small amounts of other gases, mainly carbon dioxide, noble gases and water vapour. But it wasn't always like this. Here's how the past 4.5 billion years may have gone:

Phase 1 — *Volcanoes Gave Out Gases*

1) The Earth's surface was originally molten for many millions of years. It was so hot that any atmosphere just 'boiled away' into space.

2) Eventually things cooled down a bit and a thin crust formed, but volcanoes kept erupting.

3) The volcanoes gave out lots of gas. We think this was how the oceans and atmosphere were formed.

4) The early atmosphere was probably mostly CO_2, with virtually no oxygen. There may also have been water vapour, and small amounts of methane and ammonia. This is quite like the atmospheres of Mars and Venus today.

5) The oceans formed when the water vapour condensed.

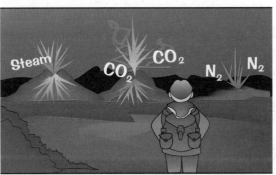

Holiday report: Not a nice place to be. Take strong walking boots and a good coat.

Phase 2 — *Green Plants Evolved and Produced Oxygen*

Holiday report: A bit slimy underfoot. Take wellies and a lot of suncream.

1) Green plants and algae evolved over most of the Earth. They were quite happy in the CO_2 atmosphere.

2) A lot of the early CO_2 dissolved into the oceans. The green plants and algae also absorbed some of the CO_2 and produced O_2 by photosynthesis.

3) Plants and algae died and were buried under layers of sediment, along with the skeletons and shells of marine organisms that had slowly evolved. The carbon and hydrocarbons inside them became 'locked up' in sedimentary rocks as insoluble carbonates (e.g. limestone) and fossil fuels.

4) When we burn fossil fuels today, this 'locked-up' carbon is released and the concentration of CO_2 in the atmosphere rises.

Phase 3 — *Ozone Layer Allows Evolution of Complex Animals*

1) The build-up of oxygen in the atmosphere killed off some early organisms that couldn't tolerate it, but allowed other, more complex organisms to evolve and flourish.

2) The oxygen also created the ozone layer (O_3) which blocked harmful rays from the Sun and enabled even more complex organisms to evolve — us, eventually.

3) There is virtually no CO_2 left now.

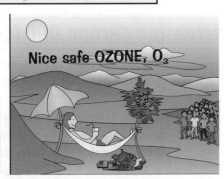

Holiday report: A nice place to be. Visit before the crowds ruin it.

The atmosphere's evolving — shut the window will you...

We've learned a lot about the past atmosphere from Antarctic ice cores. Each year, a layer of ice forms and bubbles of air get trapped inside it, then it's buried by the next layer. So the deeper the ice, the older the air — and if you examine the bubbles in different layers, you can see how the air has changed.

Chemistry 1b — Oils, Earth and Atmosphere

Life, Resources and Atmospheric Change

Life on Earth began billions of years ago, but there's no way of knowing for definite how it all started.

Primordial Soup is Just One Theory of How Life was Formed

1) The primordial soup theory states that billions of years ago, the Earth's atmosphere was rich in nitrogen, hydrogen, ammonia and methane.

2) Lightning struck, causing a chemical reaction between the gases, resulting in the formation of amino acids.

3) The amino acids collected in a 'primordial soup' — a body of water out of which life gradually crawled.

4) The amino acids gradually combined to produce organic matter which eventually evolved into simple living organisms.

5) In the 1950s, Miller and Urey carried out an experiment to prove this theory. They sealed the gases in their apparatus, heated them and applied an electrical charge for a week.

6) They found that amino acids were made, but not as many as there are on Earth. This suggests the theory could be along the right lines, but isn't quite right.

The Earth Has All the Resources Humans Need

The Earth's crust, oceans and atmosphere are the ultimate source of minerals and resources — we can get everything we need from them. For example, we can fractionally distil air to get a variety of products (e.g. nitrogen and oxygen) for use in industry:

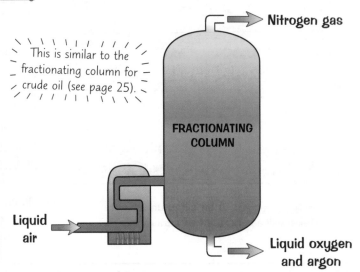

1) Air is filtered to remove dust.

2) It's then cooled to around -200 °C and becomes a liquid.

3) During cooling water vapour condenses and is removed.

4) Carbon dioxide freezes and is removed.

5) The liquified air then enters the fractionating column and is heated slowly.

6) The remaining gases are separated by fractional distillation. Oxygen and argon come out together so another column is used to separate them.

This is similar to the fractionating column for crude oil (see page 25).

Nitrogen gas

FRACTIONATING COLUMN

Liquid air

Liquid oxygen and argon

Increasing Carbon Dioxide Level Affects the Climate and the Oceans

Burning fossil fuels releases CO_2 — and as the world's become more industrialised, more fossil fuels have been burnt in power stations and in car engines. This CO_2 is thought to be altering our planet...

1) An increase in carbon dioxide is causing global warming — a type of climate change (see page 29).

2) The oceans are a natural store of CO_2 — they absorb it from the atmosphere. However the extra CO_2 we're releasing is making them too acidic. This is bad news for coral and shellfish, and also means that in the future they won't be able to absorb any more carbon dioxide.

Waiter, waiter, there's a primate in my soup...

No-one was around billions of years ago, so our theories about how life formed are just that — theories. We're also still guessing about the exact effects of global warming on things like the oceans.

Revision Summary for Chemistry 1b

Cracking alkanes, making mayonnaise, food additives and earthquakes — can they really belong in the same section, I almost hear you ask. Whether you find the topics easy or hard, interesting or dull, you need to learn it all before the exam. Try these questions and see how much you really know:

1) What is "cracking"? Why is it done?

2) Give a typical example of a substance that is cracked, and the products that you get from cracking it.

3) What kind of carbon-carbon bond do alkenes have?

4) What is the general formula for alkenes?

5) Draw the chemical structure of ethene.

6) When ethene is hydrated with steam, what substance is formed?

7) What are polymers? What kinds of substances can form polymers?

8) Give two factors which affect the physical properties of a polymer.

9) List four uses of polymers.

10) Why might polymers become more expensive in the future?

11) Why do some oils need to be distilled after they have been extracted?

12) List two advantages of cooking with oil.

13) Apart from cooking, list a use of vegetable oils.

14) What kind of carbon-carbon bond do unsaturated oils contain?

15) What happens when you react unsaturated oils with hydrogen?

16) Why do some foods contain partially hydrogenated vegetable oil instead of butter?

17) What is an emulsion? Give an example.

18) How do emulsifiers keep emulsions stable?

19) Suggest one problem of adding emulsifiers to food.

20) Give one reason why Alfred Wegener's theory of continental drift wasn't accepted for a long time.

21) What can be found beneath the Earth's crust?

22) A geologist places a very heavy marker on the seabed in the middle of the Atlantic ocean. She records the marker's position over a period of four years. The geologist finds that the marker moves in a straight-line away from its original position. Her measurements are shown in the graph on the right.

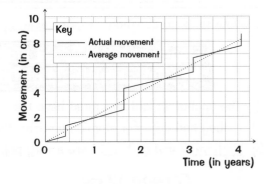

a) Explain the process that has caused the marker to move.

b)*What is the marker's average movement each year?

c)*On average, how many years will it take for the marker to move 7 cm?

23) Why can't scientists accurately predict volcanoes and earthquakes?

24) Name the two main gases that make up the Earth's atmosphere today.

25) Explain why today's atmosphere is different from the Earth's early atmosphere.

26) What is meant by 'primordial soup'?

27) Why do we fractionally distil air?

28) The burning of fossils fuels is causing a rise in the level of carbon dioxide in the atmosphere. How is this affecting the oceans and the climate?

* Answers on page 100.

Atoms, Compounds and Isotopes

Remember atoms? They're the small but important guys. Just to refresh your memory, they contain three even smaller types of particle — protons, neutrons and electrons.

Atomic Number **and** Mass Number **Describe an Atom**

These two numbers tell you how many of each kind of particle an atom has.

The Mass Number
— Total number of
protons and neutrons

$$^{23}_{11}\text{Na}$$

The Atomic Number
— Number of protons

1) The atomic number tells you how many protons there are.

2) Atoms of the same element all have the same number of protons — so atoms of different elements will have different numbers of protons.

3) To get the number of neutrons, just subtract the atomic number from the mass number. Electrons aren't counted in the mass number because their relative mass is very small.

PARTICLE	MASS
Proton	1
Neutron	1
Electron	very small

Compounds Are *Chemically Bonded*

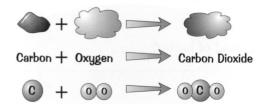

Carbon + Oxygen ⟶ Carbon Dioxide

C + O O ⟶ O C O

1) Compounds are formed when atoms of two or more elements are chemically combined together. For example, carbon dioxide is a compound formed from a chemical reaction between carbon and oxygen.

2) It's difficult to separate the two original elements out again.

Isotopes **Are the Same Except for an Extra** Neutron **or Two**

A favourite exam question: "Explain what is meant by the term isotope". LEARN the definition:

> Isotopes are: different atomic forms of the same element, which have the SAME number of PROTONS but a DIFFERENT number of NEUTRONS.

1) The upshot is: isotopes must have the same atomic number but different mass numbers.

2) If they had different atomic numbers, they'd be different elements altogether.

3) Carbon-12 and carbon-14 are a very popular pair of isotopes.

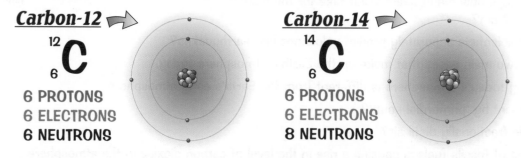

Carbon-12

$$^{12}_{6}\text{C}$$

6 PROTONS
6 ELECTRONS
6 NEUTRONS

Carbon-14

$$^{14}_{6}\text{C}$$

6 PROTONS
6 ELECTRONS
8 NEUTRONS

Will this be in your exam — isotope so...

... because obviously you'll know it as well as you know not to eat yellow snow. Anyway... it's really important you understand that an isotope is just a slight variation on the same element. Not so crazy really.

Ionic Bonding

Ionic Bonding — Transferring Electrons

In ionic bonding, atoms lose or gain electrons to form charged particles (called ions) which are then strongly attracted to one another (because of the attraction of opposite charges, + and –).

A Shell with Just One Electron is Well Keen to Get Rid...

All the atoms over at the left-hand side of the periodic table, e.g. sodium, potassium, calcium etc. have just one or two electrons in their outer shell (highest energy level). And they're pretty keen to get shot of them, because then they'll only have full shells left, which is how they like it. (They try to have the same electronic structure as a noble gas.) So given half a chance they do get rid, and that leaves the atom as an ion instead. Now ions aren't the kind of things that sit around quietly watching the world go by. They tend to leap at the first passing ion with an opposite charge and stick to it like glue.

A Nearly Full Shell is Well Keen to Get That Extra Electron...

On the other side of the periodic table, the elements in Group 6 and Group 7, such as oxygen and chlorine, have outer shells which are nearly full. They're obviously pretty keen to gain that extra one or two electrons to fill the shell up. When they do of course they become ions (you know, not the kind of things to sit around) and before you know it, pop, they've latched onto the atom (ion) that gave up the electron a moment earlier. The reaction of sodium and chlorine is a classic case:

The sodium atom gives up its outer electron and becomes an Na⁺ ion.

The chlorine atom has picked up the spare electron and becomes a Cl⁻ ion.

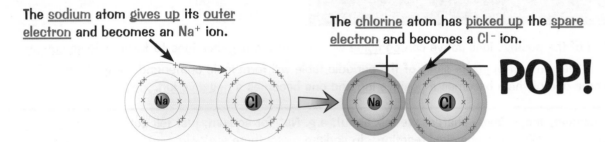

Ionic Compounds Have A Regular Lattice Structure

1) Ionic compounds always have giant ionic lattices.
2) The ions form a closely packed regular lattice arrangement.
3) There are very strong electrostatic forces of attraction between oppositely charged ions, in all directions.
4) A single crystal of sodium chloride (salt) is one giant ionic lattice, which is why salt crystals tend to be cuboid in shape. The Na⁺ and Cl⁻ ions are held together in a regular lattice.

● = Cl⁻
● = Na⁺

Ionic Compounds All Have Similar Properties

1) They all have high melting points and high boiling points due to the strong attraction between the ions. It takes a large amount of energy to overcome this attraction. When ionic compounds melt, the ions are free to move and they'll carry electric current.
2) They do dissolve easily in water though. The ions separate and are all free to move in the solution, so they'll carry electric current.

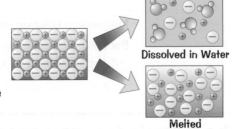

Dissolved in Water

Melted

Giant ionic lattices — all over your chips...

These guys are tough nuts to crack, but if you do crack 'em, they get all excited and start conducting electricity.

Ions and Formulas

Make sure you've really got your head around the idea of ionic bonding before you start on this page.

Groups 1& 2 and 6 & 7 are the Most Likely to Form Ions

1) Remember, atoms that have <u>lost</u> or <u>gained</u> an electron (or electrons) are <u>ions</u>.

2) Ions have the <u>electronic structure</u> of a <u>noble gas</u>.

3) The elements that most readily form ions are those in <u>Groups 1, 2, 6 and 7</u>.

4) <u>Group 1 and 2 elements</u> are <u>metals</u> and they <u>lose</u> electrons to form <u>positive ions</u>.

5) For example, <u>Group 1</u> elements (the <u>alkali metals</u>) form ionic compounds with <u>non-metals</u> where the metal ion has a 1^+ charge. E.g. K^+Cl^-.

6) <u>Group 6 and 7 elements</u> are <u>non-metals</u>. They <u>gain</u> electrons to form <u>negative ions</u>.

7) For example, <u>Group 7</u> elements (the <u>halogens</u>) form ionic compounds with the <u>alkali metals</u> where the halide ion has a 1^- charge. E.g. Na^+Cl^-.

8) The <u>charge</u> on the <u>positive ions</u> is the <u>same</u> as the <u>group number</u> of the element:

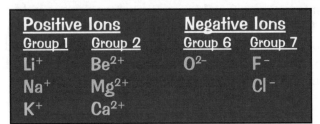

Positive Ions		Negative Ions	
Group 1	Group 2	Group 6	Group 7
Li^+	Be^{2+}	O^{2-}	F^-
Na^+	Mg^{2+}		Cl^-
K^+	Ca^{2+}		

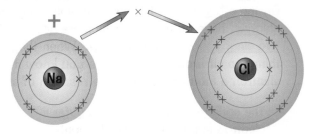

9) Any of the positive ions above can <u>combine</u> with any of the negative ions to form an <u>ionic compound</u>.

10) Only elements at <u>opposite sides</u> of the periodic table will form ionic compounds, e.g. Na and Cl, where one of them becomes a <u>positive ion</u> and one becomes a <u>negative ion</u>.

Remember, the + and − charges we talk about, e.g. Na^+ for sodium, just tell you <u>what type of ion the atom WILL FORM</u> in a chemical reaction. In sodium <u>metal</u> there are <u>only neutral sodium atoms, Na</u>. The Na^+ ions <u>will only appear</u> if the sodium metal <u>reacts</u> with something like water or chlorine.

Look at Charges to Work Out the Formula of an Ionic Compound

1) Ionic compounds are made up of a <u>positively charged</u> part and a <u>negatively charged</u> part.

2) The <u>overall charge</u> of <u>any compound</u> is <u>zero</u>.

3) So all the <u>negative charges</u> in the compound must <u>balance</u> all the <u>positive charges</u>.

4) You can use the charges on the <u>individual ions</u> present to work out the formula for the ionic compound:

> Sodium chloride contains Na^+ (+1) and Cl^- (−1) ions.
>
> (+1) + (−1) = 0. The charges are balanced with one of each ion, so the formula for sodium chloride = NaCl

> Magnesium chloride contains Mg^{2+} (+2) and Cl^- (−1) ions.
>
> Because a chloride ion only has a 1^- charge we will need <u>two</u> of them to balance out the 2^+ charge of a magnesium ion. This gives us the formula $MgCl_2$.

The formula for exam success = revision...

Remember, the + and − charges only appear when an element <u>reacts</u> with something. So, don't be fooling yourself, sodium isn't always a flashy Na^+ ion — when he's being sodium metal he's just made up of boring old <u>neutral sodium atoms, Na</u>. But wave some chlorine at him and he gets positively charged.

Electronic Structure of Ions

I heard the examiner fancies himself as a bit of an artist. This page is full of lovely drawings of <u>electronic structures</u> that should put a smile on his face.

Show the Electronic Structure of Simple Ions With Diagrams

A useful way of representing ions is by <u>drawing</u> out their electronic structure. Just use a big <u>square bracket</u> and a + or − to show the charge. A few <u>ions</u> and the <u>ionic compounds</u> they form are shown below. You need to know how to draw them:

Sodium Chloride

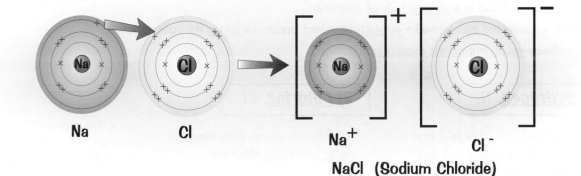

NaCl (Sodium Chloride)

Magnesium Oxide

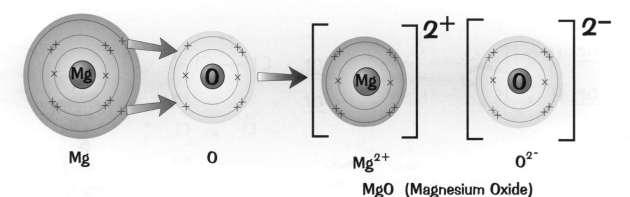

MgO (Magnesium Oxide)

Calcium Chloride

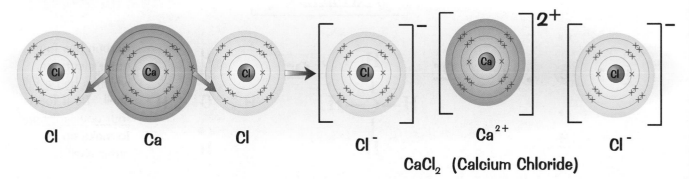

$CaCl_2$ (Calcium Chloride)

Any old ion, any old ion — any, any, any old ion...

3 ionic compounds, 3 drawings, 1 exam hall. It's like the start of a bad Game Show. Whether or not you're able to produce some lovely drawings of these bad boys all comes down to how well you've understood <u>ionic bonding</u>. (So if you're struggling, try reading the last few pages again — I know I had to).

Covalent Bonding

Some elements bond ionically (see page 43) but others form strong <u>covalent bonds</u>.
This is where atoms <u>share electrons</u> with each other so that they've got <u>full outer shells</u>.

Covalent **Bonds — Sharing Electrons**

1) Sometimes atoms prefer to make <u>covalent bonds</u> by <u>sharing</u> electrons with other atoms.
2) They only share electrons in their <u>outer shells</u> (highest energy levels).
3) This way <u>both</u> atoms feel that they have a <u>full outer shell</u>, and that makes them happy.
   Having a full outer shell gives them the electronic structure of a <u>noble gas</u>.
4) Each <u>covalent bond</u> provides one <u>extra</u> shared electron for each atom.
5) So, a covalent bond is a <u>shared pair</u> of electrons.
6) Each atom involved has to make <u>enough</u> covalent bonds to <u>fill up</u> its outer shell.
7) <u>Learn</u> these <u>seven important examples</u>:

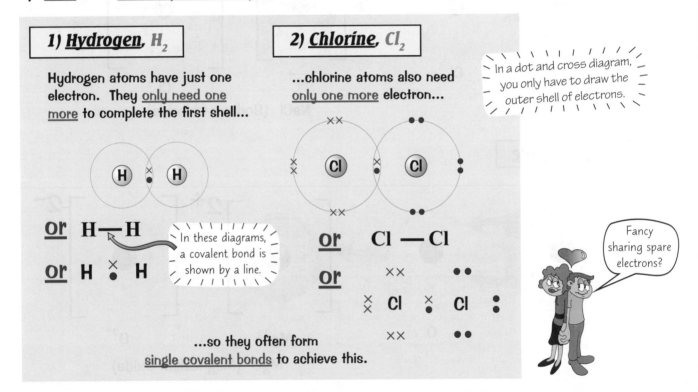

1) Hydrogen, H_2

Hydrogen atoms have just one electron. They <u>only need one more</u> to complete the first shell...

or H—H

or H ×• H

In these diagrams, a covalent bond is shown by a line.

2) Chlorine, Cl_2

...chlorine atoms also need <u>only one more</u> electron...

or Cl — Cl

or Cl × Cl

In a dot and cross diagram, you only have to draw the outer shell of electrons.

...so they often form <u>single covalent bonds</u> to achieve this.

Fancy sharing spare electrons?

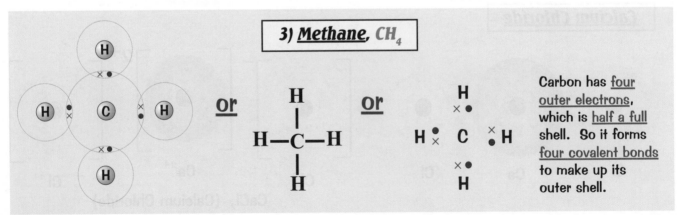

3) Methane, CH_4

or

H
|
H—C—H
|
H

or

H
×• C ×•
H × C • H
×•
H

Carbon has <u>four outer electrons</u>, which is <u>half a full shell</u>. So it forms <u>four covalent bonds</u> to make up its outer shell.

Covalent bonding — it's good to share...

There's another page of covalent bonding diagrams yet to come, but make sure you can draw the diagrams for the covalent compounds on this page first. When you've drawn a dot and cross diagram, it's a really good idea to count up the number of electrons, just to <u>double check</u> you've definitely got a full outer shell.

More Covalent Bonding

You lucky thing. There are four more examples of covalent bonding on this page — and for each compound there are three possible <u>diagrams</u>. I make that twelve diagrams in total... and just a smattering of words. So, this page is a breeze compared to others out there.

4) <u>Hydrogen Chloride</u>, HCl

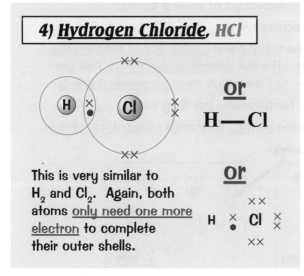

This is very similar to H_2 and Cl_2. Again, both atoms <u>only need one more electron</u> to complete their outer shells.

5) <u>Ammonia</u>, NH₃

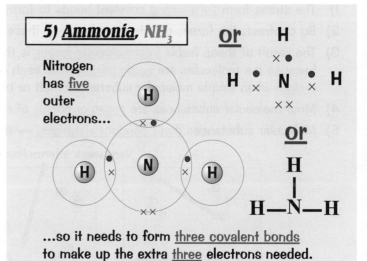

Nitrogen has <u>five</u> outer electrons...

...so it needs to form <u>three covalent bonds</u> to make up the extra <u>three</u> electrons needed.

Remember — it's only the outer shells that share electrons with each other.

6) <u>Water</u>, H₂O

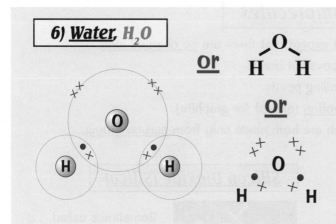

<u>Oxygen</u> atoms have <u>six</u> outer electrons. They sometimes form <u>ionic</u> bonds by <u>taking</u> two electrons to complete their outer shell. However they'll also cheerfully form <u>covalent bonds</u> and <u>share</u> two electrons instead. In <u>water molecules</u>, the oxygen <u>shares</u> electrons with the two H atoms.

7) <u>Oxygen</u>, O₂

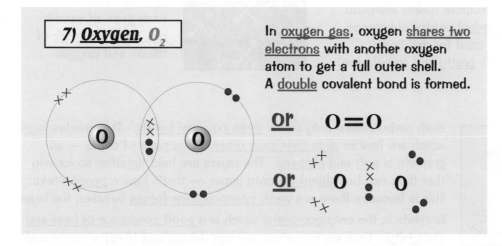

In <u>oxygen gas</u>, oxygen <u>shares two electrons</u> with another oxygen atom to get a full outer shell. A <u>double</u> covalent bond is formed.

<u>The name's Bond, Covalent Bond...</u>

Make sure you learn these seven really basic examples and <u>why they work</u>. Every atom wants a full outer shell, and they can get that either by becoming an <u>ion</u> (see page 43) or by <u>sharing electrons</u>. Once you understand that, you should be able to apply it to any example they give you in the exam.

Covalent Substances: Two Kinds

Substances with <u>covalent bonds</u> (electron sharing) can either be <u>simple molecules</u> or <u>giant structures</u>.

Simple *Molecular* Substances

1) The atoms form <u>very strong</u> covalent bonds to form <u>small</u> molecules of several atoms.

2) By contrast, the forces of attraction <u>between</u> these molecules are <u>very weak</u>.

3) The result of these feeble <u>intermolecular forces</u> is that the <u>melting</u> and <u>boiling points</u> are <u>very low</u>, because the molecules are <u>easily parted</u> from each other. It's the <u>intermolecular forces</u> that get <u>broken</u> when simple molecular substances melt or boil — <u>not</u> the much <u>stronger covalent bonds</u>.

4) Most molecular substances are <u>gases or liquids</u> at room temperature, but they can be <u>solids</u>.

5) Molecular substances <u>don't conduct electricity</u> — there are <u>no ions</u> so there's <u>no electrical charge</u>.

Very weak intermolecular forces

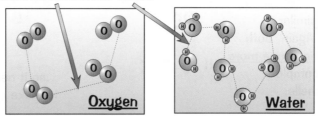

Chlorine   Oxygen   Water

Giant Covalent *Structures Are* Macromolecules

1) These are similar to giant ionic structures (lattices) <u>except</u> that there are <u>no charged ions</u>.

2) <u>All</u> the atoms are <u>bonded</u> to <u>each other</u> by <u>strong</u> covalent bonds.

3) This means that they have <u>very high</u> melting and boiling points.

4) They <u>don't conduct electricity</u> — not even when <u>molten</u> (except for graphite).

5) The <u>main examples</u> are <u>diamond</u> and <u>graphite</u>, which are both made only from <u>carbon atoms</u>, and <u>silicon dioxide</u> (silica).

Diamond

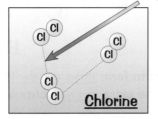

Each carbon atom forms <u>four covalent bonds</u> in a <u>very rigid</u> giant covalent structure.
This structure makes diamond the <u>hardest</u> natural substance, so it's used for drill tips.
And it's <u>pretty</u> and <u>sparkly</u> too.

Silicon Dioxide (Silica)

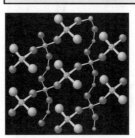

Sometimes called <u>silica</u>, this is what <u>sand</u> is made of. Each grain of sand is <u>one giant structure</u> of silicon and oxygen.

Graphite

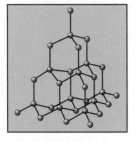

Each carbon atom only forms <u>three covalent bonds</u>. This creates <u>layers</u> which are free to <u>slide over each other</u>, like a pack of cards — so graphite is <u>soft</u> and <u>slippery</u>. The layers are held together so loosely that they can be <u>rubbed off</u> onto paper — that's how a <u>pencil</u> works. This is because there are <u>weak intermolecular forces</u> between the layers.

Graphite is the only <u>non-metal</u> which is a <u>good conductor of heat and electricity</u>. Each carbon atom has one <u>delocalised</u> (free) electron and it's these free electrons that <u>conduct</u> heat and electricity.

Carbon is a girl's best friend...

The <u>two different types</u> of covalent substance are very different — make sure you know about them both.
You should be able to recognise a <u>giant structure</u> by looking at diagrams of its <u>bonding</u>.

Metallic Structures

Ever wondered what makes <u>metals</u> tick? Well, either way, this is the page for you.

Metal Properties <u>**Are All Due to the**</u> Sea of Free Electrons

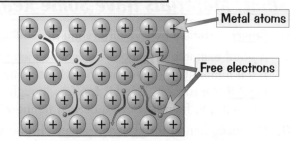

1) <u>Metals</u> also consist of a <u>giant structure</u>.

2) <u>Metallic bonds</u> involve the all-important '<u>free electrons</u>' which produce <u>all</u> the properties of metals. These delocalised (free) electrons come from the <u>outer shell</u> of <u>every</u> metal atom in the structure.

3) These electrons are <u>free to move</u> through the whole structure and so metals are good conductors of <u>heat and electricity</u>.

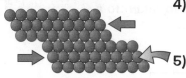

4) These electrons also <u>hold</u> the <u>atoms</u> together in a <u>regular</u> structure. There are strong forces of <u>electrostatic attraction</u> between the <u>positive metal ions</u> and the <u>negative electrons</u>.

5) They also allow the layers of atoms to <u>slide</u> over each other, allowing metals to be <u>bent</u> and <u>shaped</u>.

Alloys <u>**are**</u> Harder <u>**Than**</u> Pure Metals

1) <u>Pure metals</u> often aren't quite right for certain jobs. So scientists <u>mix two or more metals together</u> — creating an <u>alloy</u> with the properties they want.

2) Different elements have <u>different sized atoms</u>. So when another metal is mixed with a pure metal, the new metal atoms will <u>distort</u> the layers of metal atoms, making it more difficult for them to slide over each other. So alloys are <u>harder</u>.

Identifying <u>**the Structure of a Substance**</u> by Its Properties

You should be able to easily <u>identify</u> most substances just by the way they <u>behave</u> as either:

That's the guy.

- <u>giant ionic</u>,
- <u>simple molecular</u>,
- <u>giant covalent</u>,
- or <u>giant metallic</u>.

The way they might test you in the Exam is by describing the <u>physical properties</u> of a substance and asking you to decide <u>which type of structure</u> it has. Try this one:

<u>Example</u>: Four substances were tested for various properties with the following results:

Substance	Melting point (°C)	Boiling point (°C)	Good electrical conductor?
A	−218.4	−182.96	No
B	1535	2750	Yes
C	1410	2355	No
D	801	1413	When molten

Identify the structure of each substance. (Answers on page 100.)

A few free electrons and my knees have gone all bendy...

You have to be able to identify the structure of <u>any</u> substance based on its properties — and explain <u>why</u>.

New Materials

New materials are continually being developed, with new properties. The two groups of materials you really need to know about are smart materials and nanoparticles.

Smart Materials Have Some Really Weird Properties

1) Smart materials behave differently depending on the conditions, e.g. temperature.

2) A good example is nitinol — a "shape memory alloy".
   It's a metal alloy (about half nickel, half titanium) but when it's cool you can bend it and twist it like rubber. Bend it too far, though, and it stays bent. But here's the really clever bit — if you heat it above a certain temperature, it goes back to a "remembered" shape.

3) It's really handy for glasses frames. If you accidentally bend them, you can just pop them into a bowl of hot water and they'll jump back into shape.

4) Nitinol is also used for dental braces. In the mouth it warms and tries to return to a 'remembered' shape, and so it gently pulls the teeth with it.

Nanoparticles Are Really Really Really Really Tiny

...smaller than that.

1) Really tiny particles, 1–100 nanometres across, are called 'nanoparticles' (1 nm = 0.000 000 001 m).

2) Nanoparticles contain roughly a few hundred atoms.

3) Nanoparticles include fullerenes. These are molecules of carbon, shaped like hollow balls or closed tubes. The carbon atoms are arranged in hexagonal rings. Different fullerenes contain different numbers of carbon atoms.

4) A nanoparticle has very different properties from the 'bulk' chemical that it's made from — e.g. fullerenes have different properties from big lumps of carbon.

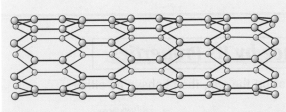

1) Fullerenes can be joined together to form nanotubes — teeny tiny hollow carbon tubes, a few nanometres across.

2) All those covalent bonds make carbon nanotubes very strong. They can be used to reinforce graphite in tennis rackets.

5) Using nanoparticles is known as nanoscience. Many new uses of nanoparticles are being developed:

- They have a huge surface area to volume ratio, so they could help make new industrial catalysts (see page 63).

- You can use nanoparticles to make sensors to detect one type of molecule and nothing else. These highly specific sensors are already being used to test water purity.

- Nanotubes can be used to make stronger, lighter building materials.

- New cosmetics, e.g. sun tan cream and deodorant, have been made using nanoparticles. The small particles do their job but don't leave white marks on the skin.

- Nanomedicine is a hot topic. The idea is that tiny fullerenes are absorbed more easily by the body than most particles. This means they could deliver drugs right into the cells where they're needed.

- New lubricant coatings are being developed using fullerenes. These coatings reduce friction a bit like ball bearings and could be used in all sorts of places from artificial joints to gears.

- Nanotubes conduct electricity, so they can be used in tiny electric circuits for computer chips.

Bendy specs, tennis rackets and computer chips — cool...

Some nanoparticles have really unexpected properties. Silver's normally very unreactive, but silver nanoparticles can kill bacteria. Cool. On the flipside, we also need to watch out for any unexpected harmful properties.

Polymers

There's plastic and there's... well, plastic. You wouldn't want to make a chair with the same plastic that gets used for flimsy old carrier bags. But whatever the plastic, it's always a polymer.

Forces Between Molecules Determine the Properties of Plastics

Strong covalent bonds hold the atoms together in long chains. But it's the bonds between the different molecule chains that determine the properties of the plastic.

Weak Forces:
Individual tangled chains of polymers, held together by weak intermolecular forces, are free to slide over each other.

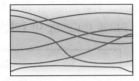

THERMOSOFTENING POLYMERS don't have cross-linking between chains. The forces between the chains are really easy to overcome, so it's dead easy to melt the plastic. When it cools, the polymer hardens into a new shape. You can melt these plastics and remould them as many times as you like.

Strong Forces:
Some plastics have stronger intermolecular forces between the polymer chains, called crosslinks, that hold the chains firmly together.

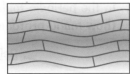

THERMOSETTING POLYMERS have crosslinks. These hold the chains together in a solid structure. The polymer doesn't soften when it's heated. Thermosetting polymers are the tough guys of the plastic world. They're strong, hard and rigid.

How You Make a Polymer Affects Its Properties

1) The starting materials and reaction conditions will both affect the properties of a polymer.

2) Two types of polythene can be made using different conditions:

- Low density (LD) polythene is made by heating ethene to about 200 °C under high pressure. It's flexible and is used for bags and bottles.

- High density (HD) polythene is made at a lower temperature and pressure (with a catalyst). It's more rigid and is used for water tanks and drainpipes.

The Use of a Plastic Depends on Its Properties

You might need to answer a question like this one in the exam.

Choose from the table the plastic that would be best suited for making:

a) a disposable cup for hot drinks,

b) clothing,

c) a measuring cylinder.

Give reasons for each choice.

Plastic	Cost	Resistance to chemicals	Melting point	Transparency	Rigidity	Can be made into fibres
W	High	High	High	Low	High	No
X	Low	Low	Low	Low	Low	Yes
Y	High	High	High	High	High	No
Z	Low	Low	High	High	High	No

Answers

a) Z — low cost (disposable) and high melting point (for hot drinks),

b) X — flexible (essential for clothing) and able to be made into fibres (clothing is usually woven),

c) Y — transparent and resistant to chemicals (you need to be able to see the liquid inside and the liquid and measuring cylinder mustn't react with each other).

Platinum cards — my favourite sort of plastic...

You need to learn the properties of thermosoftening and thermosetting polymers. But you also might be given information about the properties of a certain polymer and have to explain why it's suited to its use.

Relative Formula Mass

The biggest trouble with relative atomic mass and relative formula mass is that they sound so blood-curdling. Take a few deep breaths, and just enjoy, as the mists slowly clear...

Relative Atomic Mass, A_r — Easy Peasy

1) This is just a way of saying how heavy different atoms are compared with the mass of an atom of carbon-12. So carbon-12 has A_r of exactly 12.

2) It turns out that the relative atomic mass A_r is usually just the same as the mass number of the element.

3) In the periodic table, the elements all have two numbers. The smaller one is the atomic number (how many protons it has). But the bigger one is the mass number or relative atomic mass.

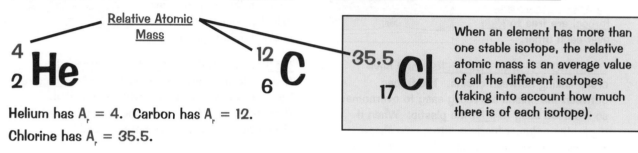

Relative Atomic Mass

$^4_2$He $^{12}_6$C $^{35.5}_{17}$Cl

When an element has more than one stable isotope, the relative atomic mass is an average value of all the different isotopes (taking into account how much there is of each isotope).

Helium has A_r = 4. Carbon has A_r = 12.
Chlorine has A_r = 35.5.

Relative Formula Mass, M_r — Also Easy Peasy

If you have a compound like $MgCl_2$ then it has a relative formula mass, M_r, which is just all the relative atomic masses added together.
For $MgCl_2$ it would be:

$$MgCl_2$$

The relative atomic mass of chlorine is multiplied by 2 because there are two chlorine atoms.

24   +   (35.5 × 2)   =   95

So M_r for $MgCl_2$ is simply 95.

You can easily get A_r for any element from the periodic table (see inside front cover), but in a lot of questions they give you them anyway. And that's all it is. A big fancy name like relative formula mass and all it means is "add up all the relative atomic masses". What a swizz, eh?

"ONE MOLE" of a Substance is Equal to its M_r in Grams

The relative formula mass (A_r or M_r) of a substance in grams is known as one mole of that substance.

Examples:
Iron has an A_r of 56.   So one mole of iron weighs exactly 56 g
Nitrogen gas, N_2, has an M_r of 28 (2 × 14).   So one mole of N_2 weighs exactly 28 g

You can convert between moles and grams using this formula:

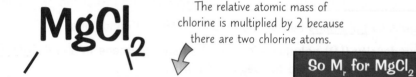

NUMBER OF MOLES = Mass in g (of element or compound) / M_r (of element or compound)

Example: How many moles are there in 42 g of carbon?
Answer: No. of moles = Mass (g) / M_r = 42/12 = 3.5 moles   Easy Peasy

Numbers? — and you thought you were doing chemistry...

Learn the definitions of relative atomic mass and relative formula mass, then have a go at these:
1) Use the periodic table to find the relative atomic mass of these elements: Cu, K, Kr, Cl
2) Find the relative formula mass of: NaOH, Fe_2O_3, C_6H_{14}, $Mg(NO_3)_2$ Answers on page 100.

Two Formula Mass Calculations

Although relative atomic mass and relative formula mass are easy enough, it can get just a tad trickier when you start getting into other calculations which use them. It depends on how good your maths is basically, because it's all to do with ratios and percentages.

Calculating % Mass of an Element in a Compound

This is actually dead easy — so long as you've learnt this formula:

$$\text{Percentage mass OF AN ELEMENT IN A COMPOUND} = \frac{A_r \times \text{No. of atoms (of that element)}}{M_r \text{ (of whole compound)}} \times 100$$

If you don't learn the formula then you'd better be pretty smart — or you'll struggle.

<u>EXAMPLE:</u> Find the percentage mass of sodium in sodium carbonate, Na_2CO_3.

<u>ANSWER:</u>

A_r of sodium = 23, A_r of carbon = 12, A_r of oxygen = 16

M_r of Na_2CO_3 = $(2 \times 23) + 12 + (3 \times 16) = 106$

Now use the formula:

$$\underline{\text{Percentage mass}} = \frac{A_r \times n}{M_r} \times 100 = \frac{23 \times 2}{106} \times 100 = 43.4\%$$

And there you have it. Sodium makes up <u>43.4%</u> of the mass of sodium carbonate.

Finding the Empirical Formula (from Masses or Percentages)

This also sounds a lot worse than it really is. Try this for an easy peasy <u>stepwise method</u>:

1) <u>List all the elements</u> in the compound (there's usually only two or three!)
2) <u>Underneath them</u>, write their <u>experimental masses or percentages</u>.
3) <u>Divide</u> each mass or percentage <u>by the A_r</u> for that particular element.
4) Turn the numbers you get into <u>a nice simple ratio</u> by multiplying and/or dividing them by well-chosen numbers.
5) Get the ratio in its <u>simplest form</u>, and that tells you the <u>empirical formula</u> of the compound.

<u>Example:</u> Find the empirical formula of the iron oxide produced when 44.8 g of iron react with 19.2 g of oxygen. (A_r for iron = 56, A_r for oxygen = 16)

<u>Method:</u>

1) <u>List the two elements:</u>	Fe	O
2) Write in the <u>experimental masses</u>:	44.8	19.2
3) <u>Divide by the A_r</u> for each element:	$44.8/56 = 0.8$	$19.2/16 = 1.2$
4) Multiply by 10...	8	12
...then divide by 4:	2	3

5) So the <u>simplest formula</u> is 2 atoms of Fe to 3 atoms of O, i.e. Fe_2O_3. And that's it done.

> You need to realise (for the exam) that this <u>empirical method</u> (i.e. based on <u>experiment</u>) is the <u>only way</u> of finding out the formula of a compound. Rust is iron oxide, sure, but is it FeO, or Fe_2O_3? Only an experiment to determine the empirical formula will tell you for certain.

With this empirical formula I can rule the world! — mwa ha ha ha...

Make sure you learn the formula and the five steps in the red box. Then try these: Answers on page 100.

1) Find the percentage mass of oxygen in each of these: a) Fe_2O_3 b) H_2O c) $CaCO_3$ d) H_2SO_4.
2) Find the empirical formula of the compound formed from 2.4 g of carbon and 0.8 g of hydrogen.

Calculating Masses in Reactions

These can be kinda scary too, but chill out, little trembling one — just relax and enjoy.

The Three Important Steps — Not to Be Missed...

(Miss one out and it'll all go horribly wrong, believe me.)

> 1) <u>Write out</u> the balanced <u>equation</u>
> 2) <u>Work out</u> M_r — just for the <u>two bits you want</u>
> 3) Apply the rule: <u>Divide to get one, then multiply to get all</u>
>   (But you have to apply this first to the substance they give you information about, and then the other one!)

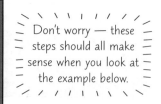
Don't worry — these steps should all make sense when you look at the example below.

Example: What mass of magnesium oxide is produced when 60 g of magnesium is burned in air?

Answer:

1) Write out the <u>balanced equation</u>:

$$2Mg + O_2 \rightarrow 2MgO$$

2) Work out the <u>relative formula masses</u>:

(don't do the oxygen — we don't need it)

$$2 \times 24 \quad \rightarrow \quad 2 \times (24+16)$$
$$48 \quad \rightarrow \quad 80$$

3) Apply the rule: <u>Divide to get one, then multiply to get all</u>:

The two numbers, 48 and 80, tell us that <u>48 g of Mg react to give 80 g of MgO</u>.
Here's the tricky bit. You've now got to be able to write this down:

> 48 g of Mg ......reacts to give.....80 g of MgO
>
> 1 g of Mg ......reacts to give.....
>
> 60 g of Mg .....reacts to give......

The <u>big clue</u> is that in the question they've said we want to burn "<u>60 g of magnesium</u>", i.e. they've told us how much <u>magnesium</u> to have, and that's how you know to write down the <u>left-hand side</u> of it first, because:

We'll first need to ÷ by 48 to get 1 g of Mg
and then need to × by 60 to get 60 g of Mg.

<u>Then</u> you can work out the numbers on the other side (shown in purple below) by realising that you must <u>divide both sides by 48</u> and then <u>multiply both sides by 60</u>. It's tricky.

÷48 48 g of Mg .... 80 g of MgO ÷48
     1 g of Mg .... 1.67 g of MgO
×60 60 g of Mg .... 100 g of MgO ×60

The mass of product is called the <u>yield</u> of a reaction. You should realise that <u>in practice</u> you never get 100% of the yield, so the amount of product will be <u>slightly less than calculated</u> (see p.55).

This finally tells us that <u>60 g of magnesium will produce 100 g of magnesium oxide</u>.
If the question had said "Find how much magnesium gives 500 g of magnesium oxide", you'd fill in the MgO side first, <u>because that's the one you'd have the information about</u>. Got it? Good-O!

Reaction mass calculations — no worries, matey...

The only way to get good at these is to practise. So have a go at these: Answers on page 100.
1) Find the mass of calcium which gives 30 g of calcium oxide (CaO) when burnt in air.
2) What mass of fluorine fully reacts with potassium to make 116 g of potassium fluoride (KF)?

Percentage Yield and Reversible Reactions

Percentage yield tells you about the <u>overall success</u> of an experiment. It compares what you calculate you should get (<u>predicted yield</u>) with what you get in practice (<u>actual yield</u>).

Percentage Yield Compares Actual and Predicted Yield

The amount of product you get is known as the <u>yield</u>. The more reactants you start with, the higher the <u>actual yield</u> will be — that's pretty obvious. But the <u>percentage yield doesn't</u> depend on the amount of reactants you started with — it's a <u>percentage</u>.

1) The <u>predicted yield</u> of a reaction can be calculated from the <u>balanced reaction equation</u> (see page 16).

2) Percentage yield is given by the formula:

$$\text{percentage yield} = \frac{\text{actual yield (grams)}}{\text{predicted yield (grams)}} \times 100$$

(The predicted yield is sometimes called the theoretical yield.)

3) Percentage yield is <u>always</u> somewhere between 0 and 100%.

4) A 100% percentage yield means that you got <u>all</u> the product you expected to get.

5) A 0% yield means that <u>no</u> reactants were converted into product, i.e. no product at all was <u>made</u>.

Yields Are Always Less Than 100%

Even though <u>no atoms are gained or lost</u> in reactions, in real life, you <u>never</u> get a 100% percentage yield. Some product or reactant <u>always</u> gets lost along the way — and that goes for big <u>industrial processes</u> as well as school lab experiments. There are several reasons for this:

1) The reaction is <u>reversible</u>:

> A <u>reversible reaction</u> is one where the <u>products</u> of the reaction can <u>themselves react</u> to produce the <u>original reactants</u>
>
> $$A + B \rightleftharpoons C + D$$
>
> <u>For example:</u>
> ammonium chloride $\rightleftharpoons$ ammonia + hydrogen chloride

This means that the reactants will never be completely converted to products because the reaction goes both ways. Some of the <u>products</u> are always <u>reacting together</u> to change back to the original reactants. This will mean a <u>lower yield</u>.

2) When you <u>filter a liquid</u> to remove <u>solid particles</u>, you nearly always <u>lose</u> a bit of liquid or a bit of solid. So, some of the product may be lost when it's <u>separated</u> from the reaction mixture.

3) Things don't always go exactly to plan. Sometimes there can be other <u>unexpected reactions</u> happening which <u>use up the reactants</u>. This means there's not as much reactant to make the <u>product</u> you want.

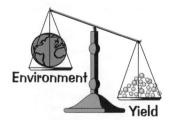
Environment | Yield

> Thinking about product yield is important for <u>sustainable development</u>. Sustainable development is about making sure that we don't use <u>resources</u> faster than they can be <u>replaced</u> — there needs to be enough for <u>future generations</u> too. So, for example, using as <u>little energy</u> as possible to create the <u>highest product yield possible</u> means that resources are <u>saved</u>. A low yield means wasted chemicals — not very sustainable.

You can't always get what you want...

A high percentage yield means there's <u>not much waste</u> — which is good for <u>preserving resources</u>, and keeping production <u>costs down</u>. If a reaction's going to be worth doing commercially, it generally has to have a high percentage yield or recyclable reactants. Learn the <u>formula</u> for working out all important percentage yield.

Chemical Analysis and Instrumental Methods

Nowadays there are some pretty clever ways of <u>identifying</u> substances, from using filter paper to machines...

Artificial Colours <u>Can Be Separated Using Paper</u> Chromatography

A <u>food colouring</u> might contain <u>one dye</u> or it might be a <u>mixture of dyes</u>. Here's how you can tell:

1) <u>Extract</u> the colour from a food sample by placing it in a small cup with a few drops of <u>solvent</u> (can be water, ethanol, salt water, etc).

2) Put <u>spots</u> of the coloured solution on a <u>pencil baseline</u> on filter paper. (Don't use pen because it might dissolve in the solvent and confuse everything.)

3) Roll up the sheet and put it in a <u>beaker</u> with some <u>solvent</u> — but keep the baseline above the level of the solvent.

4) The solvent <u>seeps</u> up the paper, taking the dyes with it. Different dyes form spots in <u>different places</u>.

5) Watch out though — a chromatogram with <u>four spots</u> means <u>at least four</u> dyes, not exactly four dyes. There <u>could</u> be <u>five</u> dyes, with two of them making a spot in the same place. It <u>can't be three</u> dyes though, because one dye can't split into two spots.

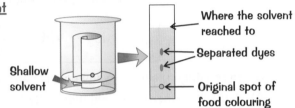

Shallow solvent

Where the solvent reached to

Separated dyes

Original spot of food colouring

Machines <u>Can Also</u> Analyse <u>Unknown Substances</u>

You can identify elements and compounds using <u>instrumental methods</u> — this just means using machines.

Advantages of Using Machines

• <u>Very sensitive</u> — can detect even the <u>tiniest amounts</u> of substances.

• <u>Very fast</u> and tests can be automated.

• <u>Very accurate</u>

Gas Chromatography <u>Can be Used to</u> Identify <u>Substances</u>

Gas chromatography can <u>separate out</u> a mixture of compounds and help you <u>identify</u> the substances present.

1) A <u>gas</u> is used to <u>carry</u> substances through a <u>column</u> packed with a <u>solid material</u>.

2) The substances travel through the tube at <u>different speeds</u>, so they're <u>separated</u>.

3) The time they take to reach the <u>detector</u> is called the <u>retention time</u>. It can be used to help <u>identify</u> the substances.

4) The recorder draws a <u>gas chromatograph</u>. The number of <u>peaks</u> shows the number of <u>different compounds</u> in the sample.

5) The <u>position of the peaks</u> shows the <u>retention time</u> of each substance.

6) The gas chromatography column can also be linked to a <u>mass spectrometer</u>. This process is known as <u>GC-MS</u> and can identify the substances leaving the column very <u>accurately</u>.

7) You can work out the <u>relative molecular mass</u> of each of the substances from the graph it draws. You just <u>read off</u> from the <u>molecular ion peak</u>.

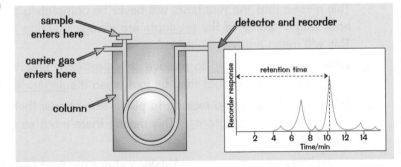

sample enters here

carrier gas enters here

column

detector and recorder

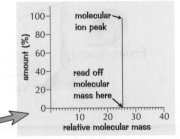

Unfortunately, machines can't do the exam for you...

Make sure you don't get the two types of chromatography muddled up... there's <u>paper</u> and then there's <u>gas</u>.

Revision Summary for Chemistry 2a

Some people skip these pages. But what's the point in reading that great big section if you're not going to check if you really know it or not? Look, just read the first ten questions, and I guarantee there'll be an answer you'll have to look up. And when it comes up in the exam, you'll be so glad you did.

1) What do the mass number and atomic number represent?
2) Draw a table showing the relative masses of the three types of particle in an atom.
3) What is a compound?
4) Define the term isotope.
5) Describe the process of ionic bonding.
6) Describe the structure of a crystal of sodium chloride.
7) List the main properties of ionic compounds.
8) What type of ion do elements from the following groups form?
   a) Group 1   b) Group 7
9)* Use information from the periodic table to help you work out the formulas of these ionic compounds:
   a) potassium chloride   b) calcium chloride
10)* Draw a diagram to show the electronic structure of an Mg^{2+} ion (magnesium's atomic number is 12).
11) What is covalent bonding?
12) Sketch dot and cross diagrams showing the bonding in molecules of:
   a) hydrogen,   b) hydrogen chloride,   c) water,   d) ammonia
13) What are the two types of covalent substance? Give three examples of each.
14) List three properties of metals and explain how metallic bonding causes these properties.
15) Explain why alloys are harder than pure metals.
16)* Identify the structure of each of the substances in the table:

Substance	Melting point (°C)	Electrical conductivity	Hardness [scale of 0 – 10 (10 being diamond)]
A	3410	Very high	7.5
B	2072	Zero	9
C	605	Zero in solid form High when molten	Low

17) Give an example of a "smart" material and describe how it behaves.
18) What are nanoparticles? Give two different applications of nanoparticles.
19) Explain the difference between thermosoftening and thermosetting polymers.
20) Define relative atomic mass and relative formula mass.
21)* Find Ar or Mr for these (use the periodic table at the front of the book):
   a) Ca   b) Ag   c) CO_2 d) $MgCO_3$ e) Na_2CO_3 f) ZnO   g) KOH   h) NH_3
22) What is the link between moles and relative formula mass?
23)*a) Calculate the percentage mass of carbon in: i) $CaCO_3$ ii) CO_2 iii) CH_4
   b) Calculate the percentage mass of metal in: i) Na_2O ii) Fe_2O_3 iii) Al_2O_3
24)*What is an empirical formula? Find the empirical formula of the compound formed when 21.9 g of magnesium, 29.2 g of sulfur and 58.4 g of oxygen react.
25)*What mass of sodium is needed to produce 108.2 g of sodium oxide (Na_2O)?
26) Describe three factors that can reduce the percentage yield of a reaction.
27) Explain how paper chromatography can be used to analyse the dyes used in a brown sweet.
28) Briefly describe how gas chromatography works.

* Answers on page 100.

Rate of Reaction

Reactions can be <u>fast</u> or <u>slow</u> — you've probably already realised that. But you need to know what affects the <u>rate of a reaction</u>, as well as what you can do to <u>measure it</u>. You'll be on the edge of your seat. Honest.

Reactions Can Go at All Sorts of Different Rates

1) One of the <u>slowest</u> is the <u>rusting</u> of iron (it's not slow enough though — what about my little MGB).

2) A <u>moderate speed</u> reaction is a <u>metal</u> (like magnesium) reacting with <u>acid</u> to produce a gentle stream of <u>bubbles</u>.

3) A <u>really fast</u> reaction is an <u>explosion</u>, where it's all over in a <u>fraction</u> of a second.

The Rate of a Reaction Depends on Four Things:

1) <u>Temperature</u>
2) <u>Concentration</u>   — (or <u>pressure</u> for gases)
3) <u>Catalyst</u>
4) <u>Surface area of solids</u>   — (or <u>size</u> of solid pieces)

Typical Graphs for Rate of Reaction

The plot below shows how the rate of a particular reaction varies under <u>different conditions</u>. The <u>quickest reaction</u> is shown by the line with the <u>steepest slope</u>. Also, the faster a reaction goes, the sooner it finishes, which means that the line becomes <u>flat</u> earlier.

1) <u>Graph 1</u> represents the original <u>fairly slow</u> reaction. The graph is not too steep.

2) <u>Graphs 2 and 3</u> represent the reaction taking place <u>quicker</u> but with the <u>same initial amounts</u>. The slope of the graphs gets steeper.

3) The <u>increased rate</u> could be due to <u>any</u> of these:

   a) increase in <u>temperature</u>
   b) increase in <u>concentration</u> (or pressure)
   c) <u>catalyst</u> added
   d) solid reactant crushed up into <u>smaller bits</u>.

You could also show the amount of reactant used up over time instead — the graphs would have the same shape.

Amount of product evolved

④ faster, and more reactants

③ much faster reaction

② faster reaction

① original reaction

Time

4) <u>Graph 4</u> produces <u>more product</u> as well as going <u>faster</u>. This can <u>only</u> happen if <u>more reactant(s)</u> are added at the start. <u>Graphs 1, 2 and 3</u> all converge at the same level, showing that they all produce the same amount of product, although they take <u>different</u> times to get there.

How to get a fast, furious reaction — crack a wee joke...

<u>Industrial</u> reactions generally use a <u>catalyst</u> and are done at <u>high temperature and pressure</u>. Time is money, so the faster an industrial reaction goes the better... but only <u>up to a point</u>. Chemical plants are quite expensive to rebuild if they get blown into lots and lots of teeny tiny pieces.

Measuring Rates of Reaction

Ways to Measure the Rate of a Reaction

The rate of a reaction can be observed either by measuring how quickly the reactants are used up or how quickly the products are formed. It's usually a lot easier to measure products forming.

The rate of reaction can be calculated using the following formula:

$$\text{Rate of Reaction} = \frac{\text{Amount of reactant used or amount of product formed}}{\text{Time}}$$

There are different ways that the rate of a reaction can be measured. Learn these three:

1) Precipitation

1) This is when the product of the reaction is a precipitate which clouds the solution.

2) Observe a mark through the solution and measure how long it takes for it to disappear.

3) The quicker the mark disappears, the quicker the reaction.

4) This only works for reactions where the initial solution is rather see-through.

5) The result is very subjective — different people might not agree over the exact point when the mark 'disappears'.

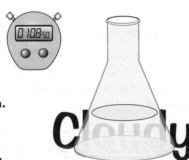

2) Change in Mass (Usually Gas Given Off)

1) Measuring the speed of a reaction that produces a gas can be carried out on a mass balance.

2) As the gas is released the mass disappearing is easily measured on the balance.

3) The quicker the reading on the balance drops, the faster the reaction.

4) Rate of reaction graphs are particularly easy to plot using the results from this method.

5) This is the most accurate of the three methods described on this page because the mass balance is very accurate. But it has the disadvantage of releasing the gas straight into the room.

3) The Volume of Gas Given Off

1) This involves the use of a gas syringe to measure the volume of gas given off.

2) The more gas given off during a given time interval, the faster the reaction.

3) A graph of gas volume against time elapsed could be plotted to give a rate of reaction graph.

4) Gas syringes usually give volumes accurate to the nearest millilitre, so they're quite accurate. You have to be quite careful though — if the reaction is too vigorous, you can easily blow the plunger out of the end of the syringe!

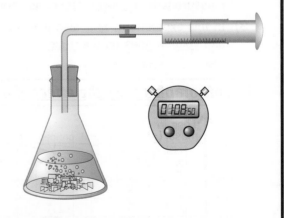

OK have you got your stopwatch ready *BANG!* — oh...

Each method has its pros and cons. The mass balance method is only accurate as long as the flask isn't too hot, otherwise you lose mass by evaporation as well as by the reaction. The first method isn't very accurate, but if you're not producing a gas you can't use either of the other two. Ah well.

Chemistry 2b — Reaction Rates, Salts and Electrolysis

Rate of Reaction Experiments

Remember: Any reaction can be used to investigate any of the four factors that affect the rate.
These pages illustrate four important reactions, but only one factor has been considered for each.
But we could just as easily use, say, the marble chips/acid reaction to test the effect of temperature instead.

1) Reaction of Hydrochloric Acid and Marble Chips

This experiment is often used to demonstrate the effect of breaking the solid up into small bits.

1) Measure the volume of gas evolved with a gas syringe and take readings at regular intervals.

2) Make a table of readings and plot them as a graph. You choose regular time intervals, and time goes on the x-axis and volume goes on the y-axis.

3) Repeat the experiment with exactly the same volume of acid, and exactly the same mass of marble chips, but with the marble more crunched up.

4) Then repeat with the same mass of powdered chalk instead of marble chips.

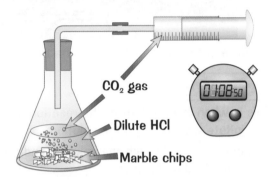

CO₂ gas

Dilute HCl

Marble chips

This graph shows the effect of using finer particles of solid

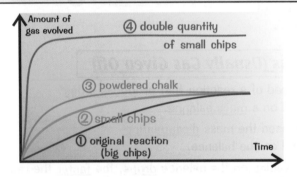

1) Using finer particles means that the marble has a larger surface area.

2) A larger surface area causes more frequent collisions (see page 62) so the rate of reaction is faster.

3) Line 4 shows the reaction if a greater mass of small marble chips is added. The extra surface area gives a quicker reaction and there is also more gas evolved overall.

2) Reaction of Magnesium Metal with Dilute HCl

1) This reaction is good for measuring the effects of increased concentration (as is the marble/acid reaction).

2) This reaction gives off hydrogen gas, which we can measure with a mass balance, as shown.

3) In this experiment, time also goes on the x-axis and volume goes on the y-axis.

(The other method is to use a gas syringe, as above.)

This graph shows the effect of using more concentrated acid solutions

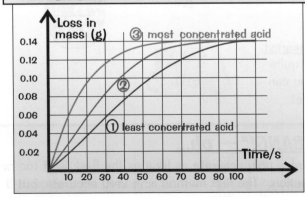

1) Take readings of mass at regular time intervals.

2) Put the results in a table and work out the loss in mass for each reading. Plot a graph.

3) Repeat with more concentrated acid solutions, but always with the same amount of magnesium.

4) The volume of acid must always be kept the same too — only the concentration is increased.

5) The three graphs show the same old pattern — a higher concentration giving a steeper graph, with the reaction finishing much quicker.

More Rate of Reaction Experiments

3) Sodium Thiosulfate and HCl Produce a Cloudy Precipitate

1) These two chemicals are both clear solutions.

2) They react together to form a yellow precipitate of sulfur.

3) The experiment involves watching a black mark disappear through the cloudy sulfur and timing how long it takes to go.

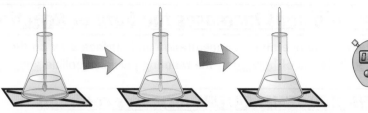

4) The reaction can be repeated for solutions at different temperatures. In practice, that's quite hard to do accurately and safely (it's not a good idea to heat an acid directly). The best way to do it is to use a water bath to heat both solutions to the right temperature before you mix them.

5) The depth of liquid must be kept the same each time, of course.

6) The results will of course show that the higher the temperature the quicker the reaction and therefore the less time it takes for the mark to disappear. These are typical results:

Temperature (°C)	20	25	30	35	40
Time taken for mark to disappear (s)	193	151	112	87	52

This reaction can also be used to test the effects of concentration. One sad thing about this reaction is it doesn't give a set of graphs. Well I think it's sad. All you get is a set of readings of how long it took till the mark disappeared for each temperature. Boring.

4) The Decomposition of Hydrogen Peroxide

This is a good reaction for showing the effect of different catalysts. The decomposition of hydrogen peroxide is:

$$2H_2O_{2\,(aq)} \rightleftharpoons 2H_2O_{(l)} + O_{2\,(g)}$$

1) This is normally quite slow but a sprinkle of manganese(IV) oxide catalyst speeds it up no end. Other catalysts which work are found in: a) potato peel and b) blood.

2) Oxygen gas is given off, which provides an ideal way to measure the rate of reaction using the good ol' gas syringe method.

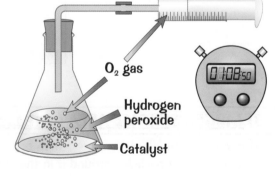

3) Same old graphs of course.

4) Better catalysts give a quicker reaction, which is shown by a steeper graph which levels off quickly.

5) This reaction can also be used to measure the effects of temperature, or of concentration of the H_2O_2 solution. The graphs will look just the same.

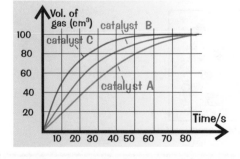

BLOOD is a catalyst? — eeurgh...

You don't need to know all the details of these specific reactions — but you do need to be able to look at graphs showing the amount of product formed (or reactant used up) over time and comment on the reaction rate.

Collision Theory

Reaction rates are explained by collision theory. It's really simple. It just says that the rate of a reaction simply depends on how often and how hard the reacting particles collide with each other. The basic idea is that particles have to collide in order to react, and they have to collide hard enough (with enough energy).

More Collisions Increases the Rate of Reaction

The effects of temperature, concentration and surface area on the rate of reaction can be explained in terms of how often the reacting particles collide successfully.

1) HIGHER TEMPERATURE increases collisions

When the temperature is increased the particles all move quicker.
If they're moving quicker, they're going to collide more often.

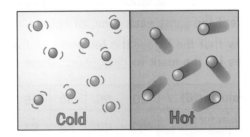

2) HIGHER CONCENTRATION (or PRESSURE) increases collisions

If a solution is made more concentrated it means there are more particles of reactant knocking about between the water molecules which makes collisions between the important particles more likely.

In a gas, increasing the pressure means the particles are more squashed up together so there will be more frequent collisions.

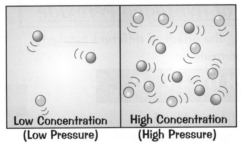

3) LARGER SURFACE AREA increases collisions

If one of the reactants is a solid then breaking it up into smaller pieces will increase the total surface area. This means the particles around it in the solution will have more area to work on, so there'll be more frequent collisions.

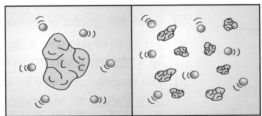

Collision theory — the lamppost ran into me...

Once you've learnt everything off this page, the rates of reaction stuff should start making a lot more sense to you. Isn't it nice when everything starts to fall into place... The concept's fairly simple — the more often particles bump into each other, and the harder they hit when they do, the faster the reaction happens.

Collision Theory and Catalysts

Without enough <u>activation energy</u>, it's game over before you start.

Faster Collisions Increase the Rate of Reaction

<u>Higher temperature</u> also increases the <u>energy</u> of the collisions, because it makes all the particles <u>move faster</u>.

Increasing the temperature causes faster collisions

Reactions <u>only happen</u> if the particles collide with <u>enough energy</u>.

The <u>minimum amount</u> of energy needed by the particles to react is known as the <u>activation energy</u>.

At a <u>higher temperature</u> there will be <u>more particles</u> colliding with <u>enough energy</u> to make the reaction happen.

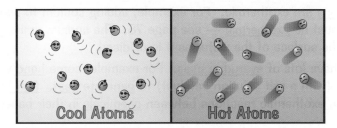

Cool Atoms   Hot Atoms

Catalysts Speed Up Reactions

Many reactions can be <u>speeded up</u> by adding a <u>catalyst</u>.

A <u>catalyst</u> is a substance which <u>speeds up</u> a reaction, without being <u>changed</u> or <u>used up</u> in the reaction.

A <u>solid catalyst</u> works by giving the <u>reacting particles</u> a <u>surface</u> to <u>stick to</u>.
This increases the number of <u>successful collisions</u> (and so speeds the reaction up).

Catalysts Help Reduce Costs in Industrial Reactions

1) Catalysts are <u>very important</u> for <u>commercial reasons</u> — most industrial reactions use them.

2) <u>Catalysts</u> increase the rate of the reaction, which saves a lot of <u>money</u> simply because the plant doesn't need to operate for <u>as long</u> to produce the <u>same amount</u> of stuff.

3) Alternatively, a catalyst will allow the reaction to work at a <u>much lower temperature</u>. That reduces the <u>energy</u> used up in the reaction (the <u>energy cost</u>), which is good for <u>sustainable development</u> (see page 55) and can save a lot of money too.

4) There are <u>disadvantages</u> to using catalysts, though.

5) They can be very expensive to buy, and often need to be removed from the product and cleaned. They never get <u>used up</u> in the reaction though, so once you've got them you can use them <u>over and over</u> again.

6) Different <u>reactions</u> use different <u>catalysts</u>, so if you make <u>more than one product</u> at your plant, you'll probably need to buy different catalysts for them.

7) Catalysts can be 'poisoned' by impurities, so they <u>stop working</u>, e.g. sulfur impurities can poison the iron catalyst used in the Haber process (used to make ammonia for fertilisers). That means you have to keep your reaction mixture very <u>clean</u>.

Catalysts are like great jokes — they can be used over and over...

And they're not only used in <u>industry</u>... every useful chemical reaction in the human body is catalysed by a <u>biological catalyst</u> (an enzyme). If the reactions in the body were just left to their own devices, they'd take so long to happen, we couldn't exist. Quite handy then, these catalysts.

Energy Transfer in Reactions

Whenever chemical reactions occur <u>energy</u> is <u>transferred to</u> or <u>from</u> the <u>surroundings</u>.

In an <u>Exothermic</u> Reaction, Heat is <u>Given Out</u>

An <u>EXOTHERMIC</u> <u>reaction</u> is one which <u>transfers energy</u> to the surroundings, usually in the form of <u>heat</u> and usually shown by a <u>rise in temperature</u>.

1) The best example of an <u>exothermic</u> reaction is <u>burning fuels</u> — also called <u>COMBUSTION</u>. This gives out a lot of heat — it's very exothermic.

2) <u>Neutralisation reactions</u> (acid + alkali) are also exothermic — see page 65.

3) Many <u>oxidation reactions</u> are exothermic. For example, adding sodium to water <u>produces heat</u>, so it must be <u>exothermic</u> — see page 75. The sodium emits <u>heat</u> and moves about on the surface of the water as it is oxidised.

4) Exothermic reactions have lots of <u>everyday uses</u>. For example, some <u>hand warmers</u> use the exothermic <u>oxidation of iron</u> in air (with a salt solution catalyst) to generate <u>heat</u>. <u>Self heating cans</u> of hot chocolate and coffee also rely on exothermic reactions between <u>chemicals</u> in their bases.

In an <u>Endothermic</u> Reaction, Heat is <u>Taken In</u>

An <u>ENDOTHERMIC</u> <u>reaction</u> is one which <u>takes in energy</u> from the surroundings, usually in the form of <u>heat</u> and is usually shown by a <u>fall in temperature</u>.

Endothermic reactions are much <u>less common</u>. <u>Thermal decompositions</u> are a good example:

Heat must be supplied to make calcium carbonate <u>decompose</u> to make quicklime.

$$CaCO_3 \rightarrow CaO + CO_2$$

Endothermic reactions also have everyday uses. For example, some <u>sports injury packs</u> use endothermic reactions — they <u>take in heat</u> and the pack becomes very <u>cold</u>. More <u>convenient</u> than carrying ice around.

Reversible Reactions <u>Can Be</u> Endothermic <u>and</u> Exothermic

In reversible reactions (see page 55), if the reaction is <u>endothermic</u> in <u>one direction</u>, it will be <u>exothermic</u> in the <u>other direction</u>. The <u>energy absorbed</u> by the endothermic reaction is <u>equal</u> to the <u>energy released</u> during the exothermic reaction. A good example is the <u>thermal decomposition of hydrated copper sulfate</u>.

endothermic

hydrated copper sulfate ⇌ anhydrous copper sulfate + water

exothermic

"Anhydrous" just means "without water", and "hydrated" means "with water".

1) If you <u>heat blue hydrated</u> copper(II) sulfate crystals it drives the water off and leaves <u>white anhydrous</u> copper(II) sulfate powder. This is endothermic.

Water vapour

2) If you then <u>add</u> a couple of drops of <u>water</u> to the <u>white powder</u> you get the <u>blue crystals</u> back again. This is exothermic.

<u>Right, so burning gives out heat — really...</u>

This whole energy transfer thing is a fairly simple idea — don't be put off by the long words. Remember, "exo-" = <u>exit</u>, "-thermic" = <u>heat</u>, so an exothermic reaction is one that <u>gives out</u> heat. And "<u>endo</u>-" = erm... the other one. Okay, so there's no easy way to remember that one. Tough.

Acids and Alkalis

Testing the pH of a solution means using an <u>indicator</u> — and that means pretty <u>colours</u>...

The <u>pH Scale</u> <u>Goes From</u> 0 to 14

1) The <u>pH scale</u> is a measure of how <u>acidic</u> or <u>alkaline</u> a solution is.
2) The <u>strongest acid</u> has <u>pH 0</u>. The <u>strongest alkali</u> has <u>pH 14</u>.
3) A <u>neutral</u> substance has <u>pH 7</u> (e.g. pure water).

| pH 0 | 1 | 2 | 3 | 4 | 5 | 6 | 7 | 8 | 9 | 10 | 11 | 12 | 13 | 14 |

$\longleftarrow$ ACIDS | ALKALIS $\longrightarrow$

NEUTRAL

car battery acid, stomach acid   vinegar, lemon juice   acid rain   normal rain   pure water   washing-up liquid   pancreatic juice   soap powder   bleach   caustic soda (drain cleaner)

An <u>Indicator</u> <u>is Just a</u> <u>Dye</u> <u>That Changes</u> <u>Colour</u>

The dye in the indicator <u>changes colour</u> depending on whether it's <u>above or below a certain pH</u>.
<u>Universal indicator</u> is a <u>combination of dyes</u> which gives the colours shown above.
It's very useful for <u>estimating</u> the pH of a solution.

Acids <u>and</u> Bases <u>Neutralise Each Other</u>

An <u>ACID</u> is a substance with a pH of less than 7. Acids form <u>H^+ ions</u> in <u>water</u>.
A <u>BASE</u> is a substance with a pH of greater than 7.
An <u>ALKALI</u> is a base that <u>dissolves in water</u>. Alkalis form <u>OH^- ions</u> in <u>water</u>.
So, <u>H^+</u> ions make solutions <u>acidic</u> and <u>OH^-</u> ions make them <u>alkaline</u>.

The reaction between acids and bases is called <u>neutralisation</u>. Make sure you learn it:

$$\text{acid} + \text{base} \rightarrow \text{salt} + \text{water}$$

Neutralisation can also be seen in terms of <u>H^+</u> and <u>OH^- ions</u> like this, so learn it too:

$$H^+_{(aq)} + OH^-_{(aq)} \rightarrow H_2O_{(l)}$$

Hydrogen (H^+) ions react with hydroxide (OH^-) ions to produce water.

When an acid neutralises a base (or vice versa), the <u>products</u> are <u>neutral</u>, i.e. they have a <u>pH of 7</u>.
An indicator can be used to show that a neutralisation reaction is over (Universal indicator will go green).

State Symbols <u>Tell You What</u> Physical State <u>It's In</u>

These are easy enough, <u>so make sure you know them</u> — especially aq (aqueous).

| (s) — Solid | (l) — Liquid | (g) — Gas | (aq) — Dissolved in water |

E.g. $\quad 2Mg_{(s)} + O_{2(g)} \rightarrow 2MgO_{(s)}$

Interesting(ish) fact — your skin is slightly acidic (pH 5.5)...

The neutralisation reaction's a great one to know. If you have <u>indigestion</u>, it's because you've got too much hydrochloric acid in your stomach. Indigestion tablets contain bases that neutralise some of the acid.

Acids Reacting With Metals

Sadly, the <u>salts</u> on this page aren't the sort you'd want to go putting on your fish 'n' chips.

<u>Metals</u> **React With** <u>Acids</u> **to Give** <u>Salts</u>

Acid + Metal → Salt + Hydrogen

That's written big 'cos it's kinda worth remembering.   Here's the <u>typical experiment</u>:

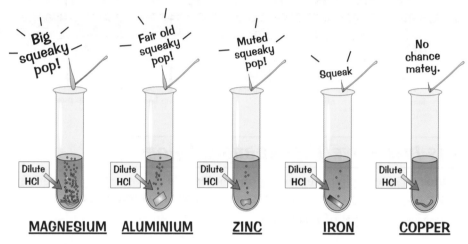

Big squeaky pop!   Fair old squeaky pop!   Muted squeaky pop!   Squeak   No chance matey.

Dilute HCl   Dilute HCl   Dilute HCl   Dilute HCl   Dilute HCl

MAGNESIUM   ALUMINIUM   ZINC   IRON   COPPER

1) The more <u>reactive</u> the metal, the <u>faster</u> the reaction will go — very reactive metals (e.g. sodium) react <u>explosively</u>.

2) <u>Copper</u> does <u>not</u> react with dilute acids <u>at all</u> — because it's <u>less</u> reactive than <u>hydrogen</u>.

3) The <u>speed</u> of reaction is indicated by the <u>rate</u> at which the <u>bubbles</u> of hydrogen are given off.

4) The <u>hydrogen</u> is confirmed by the <u>burning splint test</u> giving the notorious 'squeaky pop'.

5) The <u>name</u> of the <u>salt</u> produced depends on which <u>metal</u> is used, and which <u>acid</u> is used:

<u>Hydrochloric Acid Will Always Produce Chloride Salts:</u>

$2HCl + Mg \rightarrow MgCl_2 + H_2$ (Magnesium chloride)

$6HCl + 2Al \rightarrow 2AlCl_3 + 3H_2$ (Aluminium chloride)

$2HCl + Zn \rightarrow ZnCl_2 + H_2$ (Zinc chloride)

<u>Sulfuric Acid Will Always Produce Sulfate Salts:</u>

$H_2SO_4 + Mg \rightarrow MgSO_4 + H_2$ (Magnesium sulfate)

$3H_2SO_4 + 2Al \rightarrow Al_2(SO_4)_3 + 3H_2$ (Aluminium sulfate)

$H_2SO_4 + Zn \rightarrow ZnSO_4 + H_2$ (Zinc sulfate)

<u>Nitric Acid Produces Nitrate Salts When NEUTRALISED, But...</u>

Nitric acid reacts fine with alkalis, to produce nitrates, but it can play silly devils with metals and produce nitrogen oxides instead, so we'll ignore it here. Chemistry's a real messy subject sometimes, innit.

<u>Nitric acid, tut — there's always one...</u>

Okay, so this stuff isn't exactly a laugh a minute, but at least it's fairly straightforward learning. Metals that are <u>less</u> reactive than <u>hydrogen</u> don't react with acid, and some metals like sodium and potassium are <u>too</u> reactive to mix with acid in a school lab — your beaker would <u>explode</u>.

Oxides, Hydroxides and Ammonia

I'm afraid there's more stuff on <u>neutralisation</u> reactions coming up...

Metal <u>Oxides</u> and Metal <u>Hydroxides</u> <u>Are</u> <u>Bases</u>

1) Some <u>metal oxides</u> and <u>metal hydroxides</u> dissolve in <u>water</u>. These soluble compounds are <u>alkalis</u>.
2) Even bases that won't dissolve in water will still react with acids.
3) So, all <u>metal oxides</u> and <u>metal hydroxides</u> react with <u>acids</u> to form a <u>salt</u> and <u>water</u>.

> Acid + Metal Oxide → Salt + Water

> Acid + Metal Hydroxide → Salt + Water

(These are <u>neutralisation reactions</u> of course)

The <u>Combination</u> of Metal and Acid Decides the <u>Salt</u>

This isn't exactly exciting but it's pretty easy, so try and get the hang of it:

hydrochloric acid	+	copper oxide	→	copper chloride	+ water
hydrochloric acid	+	sodium hydroxide	→	sodium chloride	+ water
sulfuric acid	+	zinc oxide	→	zinc sulfate	+ water
sulfuric acid	+	calcium hydroxide	→	calcium sulfate	+ water
nitric acid	+	magnesium oxide	→	magnesium nitrate	+ water
nitric acid	+	potassium hydroxide	→	potassium nitrate	+ water

The symbol equations are all pretty much the same. Here are two of them:

$$H_2SO_{4\,(aq)} + ZnO_{(s)} \rightarrow ZnSO_{4\,(aq)} + H_2O_{(l)}$$

$$HNO_{3\,(aq)} + KOH_{(aq)} \rightarrow KNO_{3\,(aq)} + H_2O_{(l)}$$

Ammonia Can Be <u>Neutralised</u> with HNO_3 to Make <u>Fertiliser</u>

<u>Ammonia</u> dissolves in water to make an <u>alkaline solution</u>.
When it reacts with <u>nitric acid</u>, you get a <u>neutral salt</u> — <u>ammonium nitrate</u>:

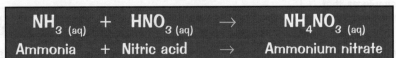

$$NH_{3\,(aq)} + HNO_{3\,(aq)} \rightarrow NH_4NO_{3\,(aq)}$$

Ammonia + Nitric acid → Ammonium nitrate

This is a bit different from most neutralisation reactions because there's <u>NO WATER</u> produced — just the ammonium salt.

<u>Ammonium nitrate</u> is an especially good fertiliser because it has <u>nitrogen</u> from <u>two sources</u>, the ammonia and the nitric acid. Kind of a <u>double dose</u>. Plants need nitrogen to make <u>proteins</u>.

There's nowt wrong wi' just spreadin' muck on it...

Not the most thrilling of pages, I'm afraid. Just loads of reactions for you to learn. Try doing different combinations of acids and alkalis. <u>Balance</u> them. Cover the page and scribble all the equations down. If you make any mistakes... <u>learn</u> it again, <u>cover</u> it up again, and <u>scribble</u> it all down again.

Making Salts

If you're making a salt it's important to know if it's soluble or not so you know which <u>method</u> to use. Most <u>chlorides</u>, <u>sulfates</u> and <u>nitrates</u> are <u>soluble</u> in water (the main exceptions are lead chloride, lead sulfate and silver chloride). Most <u>oxides</u> and <u>hydroxides</u> are <u>insoluble</u> in water.

Making Soluble Salts Using a Metal or an Insoluble Base

1) You need to pick the right <u>acid</u>, plus a <u>metal</u> or an <u>insoluble base</u> (a <u>metal oxide</u> or <u>metal hydroxide</u>). E.g. if you want to make <u>copper chloride</u>, mix <u>hydrochloric acid</u> and <u>copper oxide</u>.

Remember some metals are unreactive and others are too reactive to use for this reaction (see page 66).

E.g. $$CuO_{(s)} + 2HCl_{(aq)} \longrightarrow CuCl_{2(aq)} + H_2O_{(l)}$$

2) You add the <u>metal</u>, <u>metal oxide</u> or <u>hydroxide</u> to the <u>acid</u> — the solid will <u>dissolve</u> in the acid as it reacts. You will know when all the acid has been neutralised because the excess solid will just <u>sink</u> to the bottom of the flask.

filter paper

filter funnel

3) Then <u>filter</u> out the <u>excess</u> metal, metal oxide or metal hydroxide to get the salt solution. To get <u>pure</u>, <u>solid</u> crystals of the <u>salt</u>, evaporate some of the water (to make the solution more concentrated) and then leave the rest to evaporate very <u>slowly</u>. This is called <u>crystallisation</u>.

Making Soluble Salts Using an Alkali

1) You can't use the method above with <u>alkalis</u> (soluble bases) like <u>sodium</u>, <u>potassium</u> or <u>ammonium</u> <u>hydroxides</u>, because you can't tell whether the reaction has <u>finished</u> — you can't just add an <u>excess</u> to the acid and filter out what's left.

2) You have to add <u>exactly</u> the right amount of alkali to just <u>neutralise</u> the acid — you need to use an <u>indicator</u> (see page 65) to show when the reaction's finished. Then <u>repeat</u> using exactly the same volumes of alkali and acid so the salt isn't <u>contaminated</u> with indicator.

3) Then just <u>evaporate</u> off the water to <u>crystallise</u> the salt as normal.

Making Insoluble Salts — Precipitation Reactions

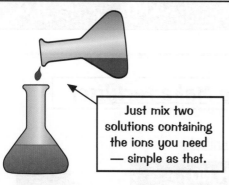

Just mix two solutions containing the ions you need — simple as that.

1) If the salt you want to make is <u>insoluble</u>, you can use a <u>precipitation reaction</u>.

2) You just need to pick <u>two solutions</u> that contain the <u>ions</u> you need. E.g. to make <u>lead chloride</u> you need a solution which contains <u>lead ions</u> and one which contains <u>chloride ions</u>. So you can mix <u>lead nitrate solution</u> (most nitrates are soluble) with <u>sodium chloride solution</u> (all group 1 compounds are soluble).

E.g. $$Pb(NO_3)_{2\,(aq)} + 2NaCl_{(aq)} \longrightarrow PbCl_{2\,(s)} + 2NaNO_{3\,(aq)}$$

3) Once the salt has precipitated out (and is lying at the bottom of your flask), all you have to do is <u>filter</u> it from the solution, <u>wash</u> it and then <u>dry</u> it on filter paper.

4) <u>Precipitation reactions</u> can be used to remove <u>poisonous ions</u> (e.g. lead) from <u>drinking water</u>. <u>Calcium</u> and <u>magnesium</u> ions can also be removed from water this way — they make water "<u>hard</u>", which stops soap lathering properly. Another use of precipitation is in <u>treating effluent</u> (sewage) — again, <u>unwanted ions</u> can be removed.

Get two beakers, mix 'em together — job's a good'n...

In the exam, you could be asked to describe <u>how</u> to make a given <u>soluble</u> or <u>insoluble</u> salt. You need to think <u>carefully</u> about what <u>chemicals</u> you'd need to get the salt you want and what <u>method</u> you'd use.

Electrolysis

Hmm, electrolysis. A not-very-catchy title for quite a <u>sparky</u> subject...

Electrolysis Means "<u>Splitting Up with Electricity</u>"

1) If you pass an <u>electric current</u> through an <u>ionic substance</u> that's <u>molten</u> or in <u>solution</u>, it breaks down into the <u>elements</u> it's made of. This is called <u>electrolysis</u>.

2) It requires a <u>liquid</u> to <u>conduct</u> the <u>electricity</u>, called the <u>electrolyte</u>.

3) Electrolytes contain <u>free ions</u> — they're usually the <u>molten</u> or <u>dissolved ionic substance</u>.

4) In either case it's the <u>free ions</u> which <u>conduct</u> the electricity and allow the whole thing to work.

5) For an electrical circuit to be complete, there's got to be a <u>flow of electrons</u>. Electrons are taken <u>away from</u> ions at the <u>positive electrode</u> and <u>given to</u> other ions at the <u>negative electrode</u>. As ions gain or lose electrons they become atoms or molecules and are released.

NaCl dissolved

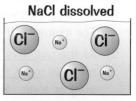

Molten NaCl

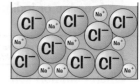

Electrolysis Reactions Involve <u>Oxidation</u> and <u>Reduction</u>

1) Back in Core Chemistry you learnt about <u>reduction</u> involving the <u>loss of oxygen</u>. However...

2) <u>Reduction</u> is also a <u>gain of electrons</u>.

3) On the other hand, <u>oxidation</u> is a gain of oxygen or a <u>loss of electrons</u>.

4) So "reduction" and "oxidation" don't have to involve <u>oxygen</u>.

5) Electrolysis <u>ALWAYS</u> involves an oxidation and a reduction.

<u>O</u>xidation <u>I</u>s <u>L</u>oss

<u>R</u>eduction <u>I</u>s <u>G</u>ain

Remember it as OIL RIG.

<u>The</u> <u>Electrolysis</u> <u>of</u> <u>Molten</u> <u>Lead Bromide</u>

When a salt (e.g. lead bromide) is molten it will conduct electricity.

<u>+ve ions</u> are attracted to the <u>–ve electrode</u>. Here they <u>gain</u> <u>electrons</u> (reduction).

<u>Lead</u> is produced at the <u>–ve electrode</u>.

Electrode (–ve)

Electrode (+ve)

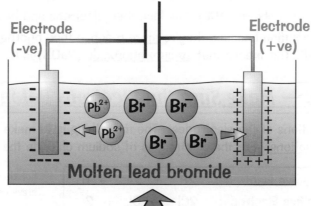

Molten lead bromide

HEAT

<u>–ve ions</u> are attracted to the <u>+ve electrode</u>. Here they <u>lose</u> <u>electrons</u> (oxidation).

<u>Bromine</u> is produced at the <u>+ve electrode</u>.

1) At the <u>–ve electrode</u>, one lead ion <u>accepts</u> two electrons to become <u>one lead atom</u>.

2) At the <u>+ve electrode</u>, two bromide ions <u>lose</u> one electron each and become <u>one bromine molecule</u>.

Faster shopping at Tesco — use Electrolleys...

Learn the <u>products</u> of the electrolysis of molten lead bromide and make sure you know which is <u>oxidation</u> and which is <u>reduction</u>. Electrolysis is used lots in <u>real life</u>, and it's nice to know how these things work, I reckon.

Electrolysis of Sodium Chloride Solution

As well as <u>molten substances</u> you can also electrolyse <u>solutions</u>. But first, a bit more about the <u>products</u>...

Reactivity Affects the Products Formed By Electrolysis

1) Sometimes there are <u>more than two free ions</u> in the electrolyte.
For example, if a salt is <u>dissolved in water</u> there will also be some <u>H^+</u> and <u>OH^-</u> ions.

2) At the <u>negative electrode</u>, if <u>metal ions</u> and <u>H^+ ions</u> are present, the metal ions will <u>stay in solution</u> if the metal is <u>more reactive</u> than hydrogen. This is because the more reactive an element, the keener it is to stay as ions. So, <u>hydrogen</u> will be produced unless the metal is <u>less reactive</u> than it.

3) At the <u>positive electrode</u>, if <u>OH^-</u> and <u>halide ions</u> (Cl^-, Br^-, I^-) are present then molecules of chlorine, bromine or iodine will be formed. If <u>no halide</u> is present, then <u>oxygen</u> will be formed.

The Electrolysis of Sodium Chloride Solution

When common salt (sodium chloride) is dissolved in water and electrolysed, it produces three useful products — <u>hydrogen</u>, <u>chlorine</u> and <u>sodium hydroxide</u>.

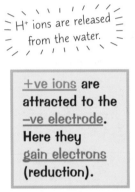

- H^+ ions are released from the water.

+ve ions are attracted to the −ve electrode. Here they gain electrons (reduction).

<u>Hydrogen</u> is produced at the <u>−ve electrode</u>.

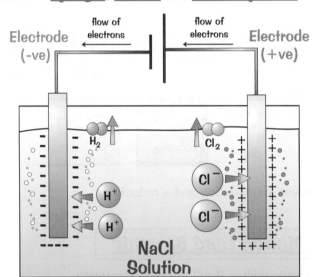

−ve ions are attracted to the +ve electrode. Here they lose electrons (oxidation).

<u>Chlorine</u> is produced at the <u>+ve electrode</u>.

1) At the <u>negative electrode</u>, two hydrogen ions accept two electrons to become <u>one hydrogen molecule</u>.

2) At the <u>positive electrode</u>, two chloride (Cl^-) ions lose their electrons and become <u>one chlorine molecule</u>.

3) The <u>sodium ions</u> stay in solution because they're <u>more reactive</u> than hydrogen. <u>Hydroxide ions</u> from water are also left behind. This means that <u>sodium hydroxide</u> (NaOH) is left in the solution.

The Half-Equations — Make Sure the Electrons Balance

Half equations show the reactions at the electrodes. The main thing is to make sure the <u>number of electrons</u> is the <u>same</u> for <u>both half-equations</u>. For the electrolysis of sodium chloride the half-equations are:

- You need to make sure the atoms are balanced too.

<u>Negative Electrode</u>: $2H^+ + 2e^- \rightarrow H_2$
<u>Positive Electrode</u>: $2Cl^- \rightarrow Cl_2 + 2e^-$
  or $2Cl^- - 2e^- \rightarrow Cl_2$

For the electrolysis of molten lead bromide (previous page) the half equations would be:
$$Pb^{2+} + 2e^- \rightarrow Pb$$
$$\text{and } 2Br^- \rightarrow Br_2 + 2e^-$$

Useful Products from the Electrolysis of Sodium Chloride Solution

The products of the electrolysis of sodium chloride solution are pretty useful in <u>industry</u>.

1) Chlorine has many uses, e.g. in the production of <u>bleach</u> and <u>plastics</u>.

2) Sodium hydroxide is a very strong <u>alkali</u> and is used <u>widely</u> in the <u>chemical industry</u>, e.g. to make <u>soap</u>.

Extraction of Aluminium and Electroplating

I bet you never thought you'd need to know so much about electrolysis — but, sadly, you do.
So get reading this lot...

Electrolysis is Used to Remove Aluminium from Its Ore

1) Aluminium's a very abundant metal, but it is always found naturally in compounds.

2) Its main ore is bauxite, and after mining and purifying, a white powder is left.

3) This is pure aluminium oxide, Al_2O_3.

4) The aluminium has to be extracted from this using electrolysis.

Cryolite is Used to Lower the Temperature (and Costs)

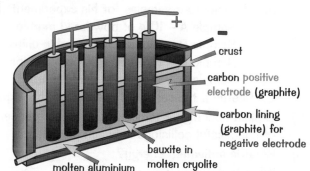

1) Al_2O_3 has a very high melting point of over 2000 °C — so melting it would be very expensive.

2) Instead the aluminium oxide is dissolved in molten cryolite (a less common ore of aluminium).

3) This brings the temperature down to about 900 °C, which makes it much cheaper and easier.

4) The electrodes are made of carbon (graphite), a good conductor of electricity (see page 48).

5) Aluminium forms at the negative electrode and oxygen forms at the positive electrode.

crust

carbon positive electrode (graphite)

carbon lining (graphite) for negative electrode

bauxite in molten cryolite

molten aluminium

> Negative Electrode: $Al^{3+} + 3e^- \rightarrow Al$ Positive Electrode: $2O^{2-} \rightarrow O_2 + 4e^-$

6) The oxygen then reacts with the carbon in the electrode to produce carbon dioxide. This means that the positive electrodes gradually get 'eaten away' and have to be replaced every now and again.

Electroplating Uses Electrolysis

1) Electroplating uses electrolysis to coat the surface of one metal with another metal, e.g. you might want to electroplate silver onto a brass cup to make it look nice.

2) The negative electrode is the metal object you want to plate and the positive electrode is the pure metal you want it to be plated with. You also need the electrolyte to contain ions of the plating metal. (The ions that plate the metal object come from the solution, while the positive electrode keeps the solution 'topped up'.)

Example: To electroplate silver onto a brass cup, you'd make the brass cup the negative electrode (to attract the positive silver ions), a lump of pure silver the positive electrode and dip them in a solution of silver ions, e.g. silver nitrate.

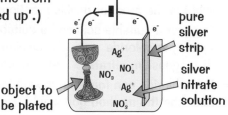

object to be plated

pure silver strip

silver nitrate solution

3) There are lots of different uses for electroplating:

- Decoration: Silver is attractive, but very expensive. It's much cheaper to plate a boring brass cup with silver, than it is to make the cup out of solid silver — but it looks just as pretty.

- Conduction: Metals like copper conduct electricity well — because of this they're often used to plate metals for electronic circuits and computers.

Silver electroplated text is worth a fortune...

There are loads of metals you can use for electroplating, but you just need to know about silver and copper plating. The tricky bit is remembering that the metal object you want to plate is the negative electrode and the metal you're plating it with is the positive electrode. Oh, and don't forget to learn about aluminium electrolysis.

Revision Summary for Chemistry 2b

Well, I don't think that was too bad, was it... Four things affect the rate of reactions, there are loads of ways to measure reaction rates and it's all explained by collision theory. Reactions can be endothermic or exothermic, and quite a few of them are reversible. And so on... Easy. Ahem.

Well here are some more of those nice questions that you enjoy so much. If there are any you can't answer, go back to the appropriate page, do a bit more learning, then try again.

1) What are the four factors that affect the rate of a reaction?

2) Describe three different ways of measuring the rate of a reaction.

3) A student carries out an experiment to measure the effect of surface area on the reaction between marble and hydrochloric acid. He measures the amount of gas given off at regular intervals.

 a) What factors must he keep constant for it to be a fair test?

 b)* He uses four samples for his experiment:
   Sample A – 10 g of powdered marble
   Sample B – 10 g of small marble chips
   Sample C – 10 g of large marble chips
   Sample D – 5 g of powdered marble
   Sketch a typical set of graphs for this experiment.

4) Explain how higher temperature, higher concentration and larger surface area increase the frequency of successful collisions between particles.

5) What is activation energy?

6) What is the definition of a catalyst?

7) Discuss the advantages and disadvantages of using catalysts in industrial processes.

8) What is an exothermic reaction? Give three examples.

9) The reaction to split ammonium chloride into ammonia and hydrogen chloride is endothermic. What can you say for certain about the reverse reaction?

10) What does the pH scale show?

11) What type of ions are always present in a) acids and b) alkalis?

12) What is neutralisation? Write down the general equation for neutralisation in terms of ions.

13) Write down the state symbol that means 'dissolved in water'.

14) What is the general equation for reacting an acid with a metal?

15) Name a metal that doesn't react at all with dilute acids.

16) What type of salts do hydrochloric acid and sulfuric acid produce?

17) What type of reaction is "acid + metal oxide", or "acid + metal hydroxide"?

18) Write a balanced symbol equation for the reaction between ammonia and nitric acid. What is the product of this reaction useful for?

19) Suggest a suitable acid and a suitable metal oxide/hydroxide to mix to form the following salts.
   a) copper chloride   b) calcium nitrate   c) zinc sulfate
   d) magnesium nitrate   e) sodium sulfate   f) potassium chloride

20) Iron chloride can made by mixing iron hydroxide (an insoluble base) with hydrochloric acid. Describe the method you would use to produce pure, solid iron chloride in the lab.

21) How can you tell when a neutralisation reaction is complete if both the base and the salt are soluble in water?

22) Give a practical use of precipitation reactions.

23) What is electrolysis? Explain why only liquids can be electrolysed.

24) Draw a detailed diagram with half equations showing the electrolysis of sodium chloride.

25) Give one industrial use of sodium hydroxide and two uses of chlorine.

26) Why is cryolite used during the electrolysis of aluminium oxide?

27) Give two different uses of electroplating.

* Answers on page 100.

History of the Periodic Table

We haven't always known as much about Chemistry as we do now. No sirree. Early chemists looked to try and understand <u>patterns</u> in the elements' properties to get a bit of understanding.

In the Early 1800s They Could Only Go on Atomic Mass

Until quite recently, there were <u>two</u> obvious ways to categorise elements:

1) Their <u>physical</u> and <u>chemical properties</u>	2) Their <u>Relative Atomic Mass</u>

1) Remember, they had <u>no idea</u> of <u>atomic structure</u> or of <u>protons</u> or <u>electrons</u>, so there was no such thing as <u>atomic number</u> to them. (It was only in the 20th century after protons and electrons were discovered that it was realised the elements were best arranged in order of <u>atomic number</u>.)

2) <u>Back then</u>, the only thing they could measure was <u>relative atomic mass</u>, and so the <u>known</u> elements were arranged <u>in order of atomic mass</u>. When this was done, a <u>periodic pattern</u> was noticed in the <u>properties</u> of the elements. This is where the name 'periodic table' comes from — ta da...

Newlands' Law of Octaves Was the First Good Effort

A chap called <u>Newlands</u> had the first good stab at arranging things more usefully in <u>1864</u>. He noticed that every <u>eighth</u> element had similar properties, and so he listed some of the known elements in rows of seven:

H	Li	Be	B	C	N	O
F	Na	Mg	Al	Si	P	S
Cl	K	Ca	Cr	Ti	Mn	Fe

These sets of eight were called <u>Newlands' Octaves</u>. Unfortunately the pattern <u>broke down</u> on the <u>third row</u>, with <u>transition metals</u> like titanium (Ti) and iron (Fe) messing it up.

It was because he left <u>no gaps</u> that his work was <u>ignored</u>. But he was getting <u>pretty close</u>, as you can see.

Newlands presented his ideas to the Chemical Society in 1865. But his work was criticised because:

1) His <u>groups</u> contained elements that didn't have <u>similar properties</u>, e.g. <u>carbon</u> and <u>titanium</u>.

2) He <u>mixed up metals and non-metals</u>, e.g. <u>oxygen</u> and <u>iron</u>.

3) He <u>didn't leave any gaps</u> for elements that hadn't been discovered yet.

Dmitri Mendeleev Left Gaps and Predicted New Elements

1) In <u>1869</u>, <u>Dmitri Mendeleev</u> in Russia, armed with about 50 known elements, arranged them into his Table of Elements — with various <u>gaps</u> as shown.

Mendeleev's Table of the Elements																
H																
Li	Be										B	C	N	O	F	
Na	Mg										Al	Si	P	S	Cl	
K	Ca	*	Ti	V	Cr	Mn	Fe	Co	Ni	Cu	Zn	*	*	As	Se	Br
Rb	Sr	Y	Zr	Nb	Mo	*	Ru	Rh	Pd	Ag	Cd	In	Sn	Sb	Te	I
Cs	Ba	*	*	Ta	W	*	Os	Ir	Pt	Au	Hg	Tl	Pb	Bi		

2) Mendeleev put the elements in order of <u>atomic mass</u> (like Newlands). But Mendeleev found he had to leave <u>gaps</u> in order to keep elements with <u>similar properties</u> in the same <u>vertical columns</u> (known as <u>groups</u>) — and he was prepared to leave some <u>very big gaps</u> in the first two rows before the transition metals come in on the <u>third</u> row.

3) The <u>gaps</u> were the really clever bit because they <u>predicted</u> the properties of so far <u>undiscovered elements</u>. When they were found and they <u>fitted the pattern</u> it was pretty smashing news for old Dmitri. The old rogue.

Julie Andrews' octaves — do-re-mi-fa-so-la-ti-do...

You need to know about how <u>Newlands</u> and <u>Mendeleev</u> tried to classify elements — and you need to be able to evaluate how well they got on. In the exam you might be given another example of the way someone has tried to classify elements and be asked to <u>compare</u> it with the ones you already know about.

The Modern Periodic Table

Chemists were getting pretty close to producing something useful.
The big breakthrough came when the <u>structure</u> of the <u>atom</u> was understood a bit better.

Not **All** Scientists **Thought the Periodic Table was** Important

1) When the periodic table was first released, many scientists thought it was just a bit of <u>fun</u>. At that time, there wasn't all that much <u>evidence</u> to suggest that the elements really did fit together in that way — ideas don't get the scientific stamp of approval without evidence.

2) After Mendeleev released his work, <u>newly discovered elements</u> fitted into the <u>gaps</u> he left. This was convincing evidence in favour of the periodic table.

3) Once there was more evidence, many more scientists realised that the periodic table could be a <u>useful tool</u> for <u>predicting</u> properties of elements. It <u>really worked</u>.

4) In the late 19th century, scientists discovered protons, neutrons and electrons. The periodic table <u>matches up</u> very well to what's been discovered about the <u>structure</u> of the atom. Scientists now accept that it's a very important and useful <u>summary of the structure of atoms</u>.

The Modern Periodic Table **is Based on** Electronic Structure

When <u>electrons</u>, <u>protons</u> and <u>neutrons</u> were discovered, the periodic table was arranged in order of atomic number.
All elements were put into <u>groups</u>.

1) The elements in the periodic table can be seen as being arranged by their <u>electronic structure</u>. Using the electron arrangement, you can predict the element's <u>chemical properties</u>.

2) Electrons in an atom are set out in <u>shells</u> which each correspond to an <u>energy level</u>.

3) Apart from the transition metals, elements in the same group have the <u>same number of electrons</u> in their <u>highest occupied energy level</u> (outer shell).

4) The <u>group number</u> is <u>equal</u> to the <u>number of electrons</u> in the <u>highest occupied energy level</u> — e.g. Group 6 all have 6 electrons in the highest energy level.

5) The positive charge of the nucleus attracts electrons and holds them in place. The <u>further</u> from the nucleus the electron is, the <u>less the attraction</u>.

6) The attraction of the nucleus is <u>even less</u> when there are a lot of <u>inner electrons</u>. Inner electrons "get in the way" of the nuclear charge, reducing the attraction. This effect is known as <u>shielding</u>.

7) The combination of <u>increased distance</u> and <u>increased shielding</u> means that an electron in a higher energy level is <u>more easily lost</u> because there's <u>less attraction</u> from the nucleus holding it in place. That's why <u>Group 1 metals</u> get <u>more reactive</u> as you go down the group.

8) <u>Increased distance</u> and <u>shielding</u> also means that a higher energy level is <u>less likely to gain an electron</u> — there's less attraction from the nucleus pulling electrons into the atom. That's why <u>Group 7 elements</u> get <u>less reactive</u> going down the group.

It's worth taking a minute (or several) to get this in your head.

You are now approaching Group III — mind the gap...

In the exam, you can be asked factual questions like "Use electronic structure to explain why caesium is more reactive than sodium" or ideas questions like "Why did scientists accept the periodic table as important?", or both. So there's no excuse for not <u>learning</u> what's on the page. Even though there is rather a lot of it...

Group 1 — The Alkali Metals

The alkali metals are <u>silvery solids</u> that have to be <u>stored in oil</u> and handled with <u>forceps</u> (they burn the skin).

Learn These Trends:

As you go <u>DOWN</u> Group 1, the alkali metals:

1) become <u>MORE REACTIVE</u>
   ...because the outer electron is <u>more easily lost</u>, because it's <u>further</u> from the nucleus.

2) have <u>LOWER MELTING AND BOILING POINTS</u>

The alkali metals have <u>LOW DENSITY</u>. In fact, the <u>first three</u> in the group are <u>less dense than water</u>.

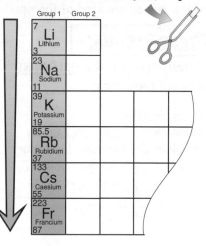

1) They are: Lithium, Sodium, Potassium and a Couple More

Know those three names real well. They may also mention <u>rubidium</u> and <u>caesium</u>.

2) The Alkali Metals All Have ONE Outer Electron

This makes them very <u>reactive</u> and gives them all similar <u>properties</u>.

3) The Alkali Metals Form Ionic Compounds with Non-Metals

1) They are <u>keen to lose</u> their one outer electron to form a <u>1+ ion</u>.

2) They are so keen to lose the outer electron there's <u>no way</u> they'd consider <u>sharing</u>, so covalent bonding is <u>out of the question</u>.

3) So they always form <u>ionic bonds</u> — and they produce <u>white compounds</u> that dissolve in water to form <u>colourless solutions</u>.

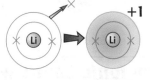

4) Reaction with Water Produces Hydrogen Gas

1) When <u>lithium</u>, <u>sodium</u> or <u>potassium</u> are put in <u>water</u>, they react very <u>vigorously</u>.

2) They <u>float</u> and <u>move</u> around the surface, <u>fizzing</u> furiously.

3) They produce <u>hydrogen</u>. Potassium gets hot enough to <u>ignite</u> it. A lighted splint will <u>indicate</u> hydrogen by producing the notorious "<u>squeaky pop</u>" as the H_2 ignites.

4) They form <u>hydroxides</u> that <u>dissolve</u> in water to give <u>alkaline</u> solutions.

$$2Na_{(s)} + 2H_2O_{(l)} \rightarrow 2NaOH_{(aq)} + H_{2\,(g)}$$
$$2K_{(s)} + 2H_2O_{(l)} \rightarrow 2KOH_{(aq)} + H_{2\,(g)}$$

The solution becomes <u>alkaline</u> (hence the name alkali metals), which changes the colour of universal indicator to <u>purple</u>.

2 trends and 4 properties — not much to learn at all...

I'm no gambler, but I'd put money on a question like this in the exam: "Using your knowledge of the Group 1 metals, describe what would happen if a piece of caesium were put into water." Just use what you know about the <u>other</u> Group 1 metals... you're going to get H_2, and a pretty violent reaction.

Group 7 — The Halogens

The 'trend thing' happens in Group 7 as well — that shouldn't come as a surprise.
But some of the trends are kind of the opposite of the Group 1 trends. Remember that.

Learn These Trends:

As you go <u>DOWN</u> Group 7, the <u>HALOGENS</u>
have the following properties:

1) <u>LESS REACTIVE</u>
   ...because it's <u>harder to gain</u> an
   extra electron, because the outer
   shell's <u>further</u> from the nucleus.
2) <u>HIGHER MELTING POINT</u>
3) <u>HIGHER BOILING POINT</u>

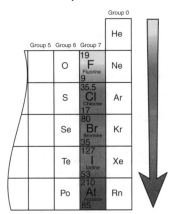

	Group 5	Group 6	Group 7	Group 0
				He
	O		$\overset{19}{\underset{9}{\text{F}}}$ Fluorine	Ne
	S		$\overset{35.5}{\underset{17}{\text{Cl}}}$ Chlorine	Ar
	Se		$\overset{80}{\underset{35}{\text{Br}}}$ Bromine	Kr
	Te		$\overset{127}{\underset{53}{\text{I}}}$ Iodine	Xe
	Po		$\overset{210}{\underset{85}{\text{At}}}$ Astatine	Rn

1) The Halogens are All Non-metals with Coloured Vapours

<u>Fluorine</u> is a very reactive, poisonous <u>yellow gas</u>.
<u>Chlorine</u> is a fairly reactive, poisonous <u>dense green gas</u>.
<u>Bromine</u> is a dense, poisonous, <u>red-brown volatile liquid</u>.
<u>Iodine</u> is a <u>dark grey</u> crystalline <u>solid</u> or a <u>purple vapour</u>.

They all exist as molecules which are <u>pairs of atoms</u>:

F_2 F F Cl_2 Cl Cl Br_2 Br Br I_2 I I

2) The Halogens Form Ionic Bonds with Metals

The halogens form <u>1⁻ ions</u> called <u>halides</u> (F^-, Cl^-, Br^- and I^-)
when they bond with <u>metals</u>, for example Na^+Cl^- or $Fe^{3+}Br^-_3$.
The diagram shows the bonding in sodium chloride, NaCl.

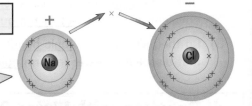

3) More Reactive Halogens Will Displace Less Reactive Ones

A <u>more reactive</u> halogen can <u>displace</u> (kick out) a <u>less reactive</u> halogen from an aqueous <u>solution</u> of its <u>salt</u>.
E.g. <u>chlorine</u> can displace <u>bromine</u> and <u>iodine</u> from an aqueous <u>solution</u> of its salt (a <u>bromide</u> or <u>iodide</u>).
<u>Bromine</u> will also displace <u>iodine</u> because of the <u>trend</u> in <u>reactivity</u>.

$$Cl_{2\,(g)} \ + \ 2KI_{(aq)} \ \rightarrow \ I_{2\,(aq)} \ + \ 2KCl_{(aq)}$$

$$Cl_{2\,(g)} \ + \ 2KBr_{(aq)} \ \rightarrow \ Br_{2\,(aq)} \ + \ 2KCl_{(aq)}$$

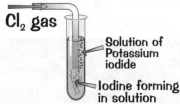

Cl_2 gas

Solution of
Potassium
iodide

Iodine forming
in solution

Polish that halo and get revising...

Once more, you don't have to be a mind-reader to be able to guess the kind of thing they're going to ask you
in the exam. My money's on something to do with <u>displacement reactions</u> — will iodine displace bromine from
some compound or other, for instance. Learn the facts... just learn the facts.

Transition Elements

Transition elements make up the big clump of metals in the middle of the periodic table.

Here they are, right in the middle of Group 2 and Group 3

| Group 1 | Group 2 | | | | | | | | | | Group 3 | Group 4 | Group 5 | Group 6 | Group 7 | Group 0 |

45 Sc Scandium 21	48 Ti Titanium 22	51 V Vanadium 23	52 Cr Chromium 24	55 Mn Manganese 25	56 Fe Iron 26	59 Co Cobalt 27	59 Ni Nickel 28	63.5 Cu Copper 29	65 Zn Zinc 30
89 Y Yttrium 39	91 Zr Zirconium 40	93 Nb Niobium 41	96 Mo Molybdenum 42	98 Tc Technetium 43	101 Ru Ruthenium 44	103 Rh Rhodium 45	106 Pd Palladium 46	108 Ag Silver 47	112 Cd Cadmium 48
57-71 Lanthanides	178.5 Hf Hafnium 72	181 Ta Tantalum 73	184 W Tungsten 74	186 Re Rhenium 75	190 Os Osmium 76	192 Ir Iridium 77	195 Pt Platinum 78	197 Au Gold 79	201 Hg Mercury 80
89-103 Actinides									

Transition elements (or transition metals) are <u>typical metals</u>, and have the properties you would expect of a 'proper' metal:

1) They're <u>good conductors</u> of heat and electricity.
2) They're very <u>dense</u>, <u>strong</u> and <u>shiny</u>.
3) Transition metals are much <u>less reactive</u> than Group I metals — they don't react as vigorously with <u>water</u> or <u>oxygen</u>, for example.
4) They're also much <u>denser</u>, <u>stronger</u> and <u>harder</u> than the Group I metals, and have much <u>higher melting points</u> (except for mercury, which is a liquid at room temperature). E.g. iron melts at 1500 °C, copper at 1100 °C and zinc at 400 °C.

Transition Metals *Often Have* More Than One Ion, e.g. Fe^{2+}, Fe^{3+}

Two other examples are <u>copper</u>: Cu^+ and Cu^{2+} and <u>chromium</u>: Cr^{2+} and Cr^{3+}.

The <u>different ions</u> usually form different-coloured compounds too:
Fe^{2+} <u>ions</u> usually give <u>green</u> compounds, whereas Fe^{3+} <u>ions</u> usually form <u>red/brown</u> compounds (e.g. <u>rust</u>).

The Compounds *are Very* Colourful

1) The <u>compounds</u> are <u>colourful</u> due to the <u>transition metal ion</u> they contain, e.g. Potassium chromate(VI) is yellow. Potassium manganate(VII) is purple. Copper(II) sulfate is blue.
2) The colours in <u>gemstones</u>, like <u>blue sapphires</u> and <u>green emeralds</u>, and the colours in <u>pottery glazes</u> are all due to <u>transition metals</u>. And weathered <u>copper</u> is a lovely colourful <u>green</u>.

Transition Metals *and Their* Compounds *All Make* Good Catalysts

1) <u>Iron</u> is the <u>catalyst</u> used in the <u>Haber process</u> (see page 82) for making <u>ammonia</u>.
2) <u>Manganese(IV) oxide</u> is a good <u>catalyst</u> for the decomposition of <u>hydrogen peroxide</u>.
3) <u>Nickel</u> is useful for turning <u>oils into fats</u> for making margarine.

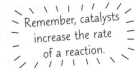
Remember, catalysts increase the rate of a reaction.

Shiny metals, pretty colours, catalysts — we've got it all...

Most <u>common everyday metals</u> are transition elements — for example, iron, nickel, copper, silver, gold...
You need to know that transition metals form ions with <u>different charges</u>, form <u>coloured</u> compounds and make good <u>catalysts</u> — oh, and you need to be able to <u>compare</u> them with the Group 1 metals.

Hardness of Water

Water where you live might be hard or soft. It depends on the rocks your water meets on its way to you.

Hard Water Makes Scum and Scale

1) With soft water, you get a nice lather with soap. But with hard water you get a nasty scum instead — unless you're using a soapless detergent. The problem is dissolved calcium ions and magnesium ions in the water (see below) reacting with the soap to make scum which is insoluble. So to get a decent lather you need to use more soap — and because soap isn't free, that means more money going down the drain.

2) When heated, hard water also forms furring or scale (mostly calcium carbonate) on the insides of pipes, boilers and kettles. Badly scaled-up pipes and boilers reduce the efficiency of heating systems, and may need to be replaced — all of which costs money. Scale can even eventually block pipes.

3) Scale is also a bit of a thermal insulator. This means that a kettle with scale on the heating element takes longer to boil than a clean non-scaled-up kettle — so it becomes less efficient.

Hardness is Caused by Ca^{2+} and Mg^{2+} Ions

1) Most hard water is hard because it contains lots of calcium ions and magnesium ions.

2) Rain falling on some types of rocks (e.g. limestone, chalk and gypsum) can dissolve compounds like magnesium sulfate (which is soluble), and calcium sulfate (which is also soluble, though only a bit).

Hard Water Isn't All Bad

1) Ca^{2+} ions are good for healthy teeth and bones.

2) Studies have found that people who live in hard water areas are at less risk of developing heart disease than people who live in soft water areas. This could be to do with the minerals in hard water.

Remove the Dissolved Ca^{2+} and Mg^{2+} Ions to Make Hard Water Soft

There are two kinds of hardness — temporary and permanent.
Temporary hardness is caused by the hydrogencarbonate ion, HCO_3^-, in $Ca(HCO_3)_2$.
Permanent hardness is caused by dissolved calcium sulfate (among other things).

1) Temporary hardness is removed by boiling. When heated, the calcium hydrogencarbonate decomposes to form calcium carbonate which is insoluble. This solid is the 'limescale' on your kettle.

e.g.
$$\text{calcium hydrogencarbonate} \rightarrow \text{calcium carbonate} + \text{water} + \text{carbon dioxide}$$
$$Ca(HCO_3)_{2(aq)} \rightarrow CaCO_{3(s)} + H_2O_{(l)} + CO_{2(g)}$$

This won't work for permanent hardness, though. Heating a sulfate ion does nowt.

2) Both types of hardness can be softened by adding washing soda (sodium carbonate, Na_2CO_3) to it. The added carbonate ions react with the Ca^{2+} and Mg^{2+} ions to make an insoluble precipitate of calcium carbonate and magnesium carbonate. The Ca^{2+} and Mg^{2+} ions are no longer dissolved in the water so they can't make it hard.

e.g.
$$Ca^{2+}_{(aq)} + CO_3^{2-}_{(aq)} \rightarrow CaCO_{3(s)}$$

3) Both types of hardness can also be removed by running water through 'ion exchange columns' which are sold in shops. The columns have lots of sodium ions (or hydrogen ions) and 'exchange' them for calcium or magnesium ions in the water that runs through them.

e.g.
$$Na_2Resin_{(s)} + Ca^{2+}_{(aq)} \rightarrow CaResin_{(s)} + 2Na^+_{(aq)}$$

('Resin' is a huge insoluble resin molecule.)

And if the water's really hard, you can chip your teeth...

Hard water — good thing or bad thing... Well, it provides minerals that are good for health, but it creates an awful lot of unnecessary expense. All in all, it's a bit of a drag. But you still need to learn it.

Hardness of Water

If you live in an area of <u>hard water</u> you might already know about it because you sometimes get a grimy layer of <u>scale</u> floating on the top of your tea and you get through more shampoo than you can shake a stick at...

You Can Use <u>Titration</u> to <u>Compare the Hardness</u> of <u>Water Samples</u>

Method

1) Fill a burette with <u>50 cm³ of soap solution</u>.
2) Add <u>50 cm³</u> of the first <u>water</u> sample into a flask.
3) Use the burette to add <u>1 cm³ of soap solution</u> to the flask.
4) Put a <u>bung</u> in the flask and <u>shake</u> for 10 seconds.
5) <u>Repeat</u> steps 3 and 4 until a <u>good lasting lather</u> is formed. (A lasting lather is one where the <u>bubbles cover the surface</u> for <u>at least 30 seconds</u>.)
6) <u>Record</u> how much soap was needed to create a lasting lather.
7) <u>Repeat</u> steps 1-6 with the other water samples.
8) Next, <u>boil fresh samples</u> of each type of water for <u>ten minutes</u>, and <u>repeat</u> the experiment.

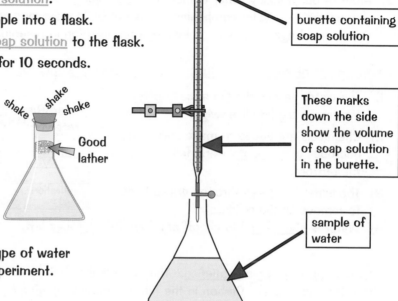

shake   shake   shake

Good lather

burette containing soap solution

These marks down the side show the volume of soap solution in the burette.

sample of water

Results

This method was carried out on <u>3 different samples of water</u> — <u>distilled</u> water, <u>local tap water</u> and <u>imported tap water</u>. Here's the <u>table of results</u>:

Sample	Volume of soap solution needed to give a good lather	
	using unboiled water in cm³	using boiled water in cm³
Distilled	1	1
Local water	7	1
Imported water	14	8

The results tell you the following things about the water:

1) Distilled water contains little or no <u>hardness</u> — only the <u>minimum</u> amount of soap was needed.
2) The sample of <u>imported water</u> contains <u>more hardness</u> than <u>local water</u> — <u>more soap</u> was needed to produce a lather.
3) The local water contains only <u>temporary hardness</u> — all the hardness is <u>removed by boiling</u>. You can tell because the same amount of soap was needed for <u>boiled local water</u> as for <u>distilled water</u>.
4) The imported water contains both <u>temporary</u> and <u>permanent hardness</u>. 8 cm³ of soap is still needed to produce a lather after boiling.
5) If your brain's really switched on, you'll see that the local water and the imported water contain the <u>same amount</u> of <u>temporary hardness</u>. In both cases, the amount of soap needed in the <u>boiled</u> sample is <u>6 cm³ less</u> than in the <u>unboiled</u> sample.

My water's harder than yours...

One thing that I've never understood is that they sell water softeners in areas that <u>already</u> have soft water. Hmm... Anyhow, the usual message here. There <u>is</u> an exam coming up, and <u>any</u> of this hard water stuff could be on it. Read through any experimental data they give you carefully — don't drop the easy marks.

Water Quality

It's easy to take water for granted... turn on the tap, and there it is — nice, clean water. The water you drink's been round the block a few times — so there's some <u>fancy chemistry</u> needed to make it drinkable.

Drinking Water Needs to Be Good Quality

1) Water's essential for life, but it must be free of <u>poisonous salts</u> (e.g. phosphates and nitrates) and harmful <u>microbes</u>. Microbes in water can cause <u>diseases</u> such as cholera and dysentery.

2) Most of our drinking water comes from <u>reservoirs</u>. Water flows into reservoirs from <u>rivers</u> and <u>groundwater</u> — water companies choose to build reservoirs where there's a good supply of <u>clean water</u>. Government agencies keep a close eye on <u>pollution</u> in reservoirs, rivers and groundwater.

<u>Water from reservoirs goes to the water treatment works for treatment</u>:

1) The water passes though a <u>mesh screen</u> to remove big bits like twigs.

2) Chemicals are added to make solids and microbes <u>stick together</u> and fall to the bottom.

3) The water is <u>filtered</u> through gravel beds to remove all the solids.

4) Water is <u>chlorinated</u> to kill off any harmful <u>microbes</u> left.

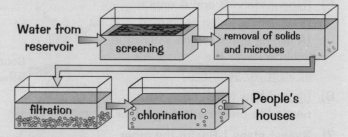

Some people <u>still aren't satisfied</u>. They buy filters that contain <u>carbon</u> or <u>silver</u> to remove substances from their tap water. Carbon in the filters removes <u>chlorine taste</u> and silver is supposed to kill bugs. Some people in hard water areas buy <u>water softeners</u> which contain <u>ion exchange resins</u> (see p.78).

<u>Totally pure water</u> with <u>nothing</u> dissolved in it can be produced by <u>distillation</u> — boiling water to make steam and condensing the steam. This process is too <u>expensive</u> to produce tap water — bags of energy would be needed to boil all the water we use. Distilled water is used in <u>chemistry labs</u>.

You'd use pure water to make a solution of (say) KBr, because you wouldn't want any other ions mucking it up.

Adding Fluoride and Chlorine to Water Has Disadvantages

1) <u>Fluoride</u> is added to drinking water in some parts of the country because it helps to <u>reduce tooth decay</u>. <u>Chlorine</u> is added to <u>prevent disease</u> (see above). So far so good. However...

2) Some studies have linked adding chlorine to water with an <u>increase</u> in certain <u>cancers</u>. Chlorine can <u>react</u> with other <u>natural substances</u> in water to produce <u>toxic by-products</u> which some people think could cause cancer.

3) In <u>high doses</u> fluoride can cause <u>cancer</u> and <u>bone problems</u> in humans, so some people believe that fluoride <u>shouldn't be added</u> to drinking water. There is also concern about whether it's right to 'mass medicate' — people can <u>choose</u> whether to use a <u>fluoride toothpaste</u>, but they can't choose whether their tap water has added fluoride.

4) <u>Levels of chemicals</u> added to drinking water need to be carefully <u>monitored</u>. For example, in some areas the water may already contain a lot of fluoride, so adding more could be harmful.

The water you drink has been through 7 people already...

Well, it's possible. It's also possible that the water you're drinking used to be part of the Atlantic Ocean. Or it could have been drunk by Alexander the Great. Or part of an Alpine glacier. Aye, it gets about a bit, does water. And remember... tap water isn't pure — but it's <u>drinkable</u>, and that's the main thing.

Reversible Reactions

A <u>reversible reaction</u> is one where the <u>products</u> of the
reaction can <u>themselves react</u> to produce the <u>original reactants</u>

$$A + B \rightleftharpoons C + D$$

In other words, <u>the reaction can go both ways</u>.

Reversible Reactions Will Reach *Equilibrium*

1) If a reversible reaction takes place in a <u>closed system</u>
   then a state of <u>equilibrium</u> will always be reached.

2) <u>Equilibrium</u> means that the <u>amounts</u> of reactants and
   products will reach a certain <u>balance</u> and stay there.
   (A '<u>closed system</u>' just means that none of the reactants
   or products can <u>escape</u>.)

3) The reactions are still taking place in <u>both directions</u>, but
   the <u>overall effect is nil</u> because the forward and reverse
   reactions <u>cancel</u> each other out. The reactions are taking
   place at <u>exactly the same rate</u> in both directions.

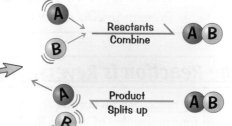

Changing Temperature and Pressure to Get More Product

1) In a reversible reaction the '<u>position of equilibrium</u>' (the relative amounts of reactants and products)
   depends <u>very strongly</u> on the <u>temperature</u> and <u>pressure</u> surrounding the reaction.

2) If you <u>deliberately alter</u> the temperature and pressure you can <u>move</u> the 'position of equilibrium'
   to give <u>more product</u> and <u>less</u> reactants.

Temperature

All reactions are <u>exothermic</u> in one direction and <u>endothermic</u> in the other.

If you <u>raise</u> the <u>temperature</u>, the <u>endothermic</u> reaction will increase to <u>use up</u> the extra heat.

If you <u>reduce</u> the <u>temperature</u>, the <u>exothermic</u> reaction will increase to <u>give out</u> more heat.

Pressure

Many reactions have a <u>greater volume</u> on one side, either of <u>products</u> or <u>reactants</u> (greater volume
means there are more gas molecules and less volume means there are fewer gas molecules).

If you <u>raise</u> the <u>pressure</u> it will encourage the reaction which produces <u>less volume</u>.

If you <u>lower</u> the <u>pressure</u> it will encourage the reaction which produces <u>more volume</u>.

<u>Adding a CATALYST doesn't change the equilibrium position:</u>

1) Catalysts speed up <u>both</u> the <u>forward</u> and <u>backward</u> reactions by the <u>same amount</u>.

2) So, adding a catalyst means the reaction reaches equilibrium <u>quicker</u>, but you end
   up with the <u>same amount</u> of product as you would without the catalyst.

Remember — catalysts DON'T affect the equilibrium position...

Changing the temperature <u>always</u> changes the equilibrium position, but that's not true of pressure.
If your reaction has the same number of gas molecules on each side of the equation, changing the pressure
won't make any difference at all to the equilibrium position (it still affects the <u>rate</u> of reaction though).

The Haber Process

This is an <u>important industrial process</u>. It produces <u>ammonia</u> (NH_3), which is used to make <u>fertilisers</u>.

<u>Nitrogen</u> and <u>Hydrogen</u> Are Needed to Make <u>Ammonia</u>

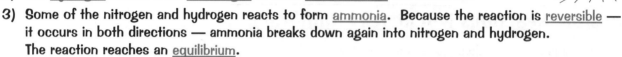

$$N_{2\,(g)} + 3H_{2\,(g)} \rightleftharpoons 2NH_{3\,(g)} \quad (+ \text{ heat})$$

1) The <u>nitrogen</u> is obtained easily from the <u>air</u>, which is <u>78% nitrogen</u> (and **21% oxygen**). ⌐ These gases are ¬ first purified.

2) The <u>hydrogen</u> comes from <u>natural gas</u> or from <u>other sources</u> like crude oil.

3) Some of the nitrogen and hydrogen reacts to form <u>ammonia</u>. Because the reaction is <u>reversible</u> — it occurs in both directions — ammonia breaks down again into nitrogen and hydrogen. The reaction reaches an <u>equilibrium</u>.

> ### Industrial conditions:
> <u>Pressure</u>: 200 atmospheres; <u>Temperature</u>: 450 °C; <u>Catalyst</u>: Iron

The Reaction is <u>Reversible</u>, So There's a <u>Compromise</u> to be Made:

1) <u>Higher pressures</u> favour the <u>forward</u> reaction (since there are four molecules of gas on the left-hand side, for every two molecules on the right — see the equation above).

2) So the pressure is set <u>as high as possible</u> to give the best % yield, without making the plant too expensive to build (it'd be too expensive to build a plant that'd stand pressures of over 1000 atmospheres, for example). Hence the <u>200 atmospheres</u> operating pressure.

3) The <u>forward reaction</u> is <u>exothermic</u>, which means that <u>increasing</u> the <u>temperature</u> will actually move the equilibrium the <u>wrong way</u> — away from ammonia and towards N_2 and H_2. So the yield of ammonia would be greater at <u>lower temperatures</u>.

4) The trouble is, <u>lower temperatures</u> mean a <u>lower rate of reaction</u>. So what they do is increase the temperature anyway, to get a much faster rate of reaction.

5) The 450 °C is a <u>compromise</u> between <u>maximum yield</u> and <u>speed of reaction</u>. It's better to wait just <u>20 seconds</u> for a <u>10% yield</u> than to have to wait <u>60 seconds</u> for a <u>20% yield</u>.

6) The <u>ammonia</u> is formed as a <u>gas</u> but as it cools in the condenser it <u>liquefies</u> and is <u>removed</u>.

7) The unused hydrogen (H_2) and nitrogen (N_2) are <u>recycled</u> so <u>nothing is wasted</u>.

(Diagram labels: H₂ and N₂ mixed in 3:1 ratio; Reaction vessel; Trays of iron catalyst; 450°C 200 atm; Unused N₂ and H₂ is recycled; Condenser; Liquid Ammonia)

The Iron Catalyst <u>Speeds Up</u> the Reaction and Keeps <u>Costs Down</u>

1) The <u>iron catalyst</u> makes the reaction go <u>faster</u>, which gets it to the <u>equilibrium proportions</u> more quickly. But remember, the catalyst <u>doesn't</u> affect the <u>position</u> of equilibrium (i.e. the % yield).

2) <u>Without the catalyst</u> the temperature would have to be <u>raised even further</u> to get a <u>quick enough</u> reaction, and that would <u>reduce the % yield</u> even further. So the catalyst is very important.

You need to learn this stuff — go on, Haber go at it...

The trickiest bit is remembering that the temperature is raised <u>not for a better equilibrium</u>, but for <u>speed</u>. It doesn't matter that the percentage yield is low, because the hydrogen and nitrogen are recycled. Cover the page and scribble down as much as you can remember, then check, and try again.

Alcohols

This page is about different types of alcohols — and that's not just beer, wine and spirits.

Alcohols *Have an* '-OH' *Functional Group and End in* '-ol'

1) The general formula of an alcohol is $C_nH_{2n+1}OH$. So an alcohol with 2 carbons has the formula C_2H_5OH.

2) All alcohols contain the same -OH group. You need to know the first 3 in the homologous series:

Methanol	Ethanol	Propanol
H | H—C—O—H | H	H H | | H—C—C—O—H | | H H	H H H | | | H—C—C—C—O—H | | | H H H
CH_3OH	C_2H_5OH	C_3H_7OH

A homologous series is a group of chemicals that react in a similar way because they have the same functional group (in alcohols it's the —OH group).

3) The basic naming system is the same as for alkanes — but replace the final '-e' with '-ol'.

4) Don't write CH_4O instead of CH_3OH — it doesn't show the functional -OH group.

The *First Three Alcohols* Have *Similar Properties*

1) Alcohols are flammable. They burn in air to produce carbon dioxide and water.
   E.g.

   $$2CH_3OH_{(l)} + 3O_{2(g)} \rightarrow 2CO_{2(g)} + 4H_2O_{(g)}$$

2) The first three alcohols all dissolve completely in water to form neutral solutions.

3) They also react with sodium to give hydrogen and alkoxides, e.g. ethanol gives sodium ethoxide and H_2.
   E.g.

   $$2C_2H_5OH_{(l)} + 2Na_{(s)} \rightarrow 2C_2H_5ONa_{(aq)} + H_{2(g)}$$

4) Ethanol is the main alcohol in alcoholic drinks. It's not as toxic as methanol (which causes blindness if drunk) but it still damages the liver and brain.

Alcohols *are Used as* Solvents

1) Alcohols such as methanol and ethanol can dissolve most compounds that water dissolves, but they can also dissolve substances that water can't dissolve — e.g. hydrocarbons, oils and fats. This makes ethanol, methanol and propanol very useful solvents in industry.

2) Ethanol is the solvent for perfumes and aftershave lotions. It can mix with both the oils (which give the smell) and the water (that makes up the bulk).

3) 'Methylated spirit' (or 'meths') is ethanol with chemicals (e.g. methanol) added to it. It's used to clean paint brushes and as a fuel (among other things). It's poisonous to drink, so a purply-blue dye is also added (to stop people drinking it by mistake).

Alcohols *are Used as* Fuels

1) Ethanol is used as a fuel in spirit burners — it burns fairly cleanly and it's non-smelly.

2) Ethanol can also be mixed in with petrol and used as fuel for cars. Since pure ethanol is clean burning, the more ethanol in a petrol/ethanol mix, the less pollution is produced.

3) Some countries that have little or no oil deposits but plenty of land and sunshine (e.g. Brazil) grow loads of sugar cane, which they ferment to form ethanol.

4) A big advantage of this is that sugar cane is a renewable resource (unlike petrol, which will run out).

Quick tip — don't fill your car with single malt whisky...

The examiners will be happy if you know the formulas, the structures, the properties and the reactions on this page. They might also give you some extra information about alcohols to evaluate... knowing the facts on this page will help you be able to do that. I know what I'd do...

Carboxylic Acids

So what if carboxylic is a funny name — these are easy.

Carboxylic Acids Have the Functional Group -COOH

1) Carboxylic acids have '-COOH' as a functional group.

2) Their names end in '-anoic acid' (and start with the normal 'meth/eth/prop').

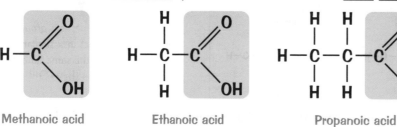

Methanoic acid
HCOOH

Ethanoic acid
CH$_3$COOH

Propanoic acid
C$_2$H$_5$COOH

Carboxylic Acids React Like Other Acids

1) They react just like any other acid with carbonates to produce carbon dioxide.

2) The salts formed in these reactions end in -anoate — e.g. methanoic acid will form a methanoate, ethanoic acid an ethanoate, etc. For example:

> ethanoic acid + sodium carbonate → carbon dioxide + sodium ethanoate

3) Carboxylic acids dissolve in water to produce acidic solutions. When they dissolve, they ionise and release H$^+$ ions which are responsible for making the solution acidic. But, because they don't ionise completely (not many H$^+$ ions are released), they just form weak acidic solutions. This means that they have a higher pH (less acidic) than aqueous solutions of strong acids with the same concentration.

The strength of an acid isn't the same as its concentration. Concentration is how watered down your acid is and strength is how well it has ionised in water.

Some Carboxylic Acids are Fairly Common

1) Ethanoic acid can be made by oxidising ethanol. Microbes, like yeast, cause the ethanol to ferment. Ethanol can also be oxidised using oxidising agents.

> ethanol + oxygen → ethanoic acid + water

If you leave wine open, the ethanol in it is oxidised — this is why it goes off.

2) Ethanoic acid can then be dissolved in water to make vinegar, which is used for flavouring and preserving foods.

3) Citric acid (another carboxylic acid) is present in oranges and lemons, and is manufactured in large quantities to make fizzy drinks. It's also used to get rid of scale (see page 78).

Carboxylic Acids are Used in Industry to Make Soaps and Esters

1) Carboxylic acids with longer chains of carbon atoms are used to make soaps and detergents.

2) Carboxylic acids are also used in the preparation of esters (see next page).

3) Ethanoic acid is a very good solvent for many organic molecules.
But ethanoic acid isn't usually chosen as a solvent because it makes the solution acidic.

Ethanoic acid — it's not just for putting on your chips...

The trickiest bit on this page is probably the bit about carboxylic acids not ionising completely in water and being weak acids. But when it comes to carbonates, they just act like any old acid — easy.

Esters

Mix an alcohol from p.83 and a carboxylic acid from p.84, and what have you got... an <u>ester</u>, that's what.

Esters *Have the Functional Group* -COO-

1) <u>Esters</u> are formed from an <u>alcohol</u> and a <u>carboxylic acid</u>.

2) An <u>acid catalyst</u> is usually used (e.g. concentrated <u>sulfuric acid</u>).

> alcohol + carboxylic acid → ester + water

$$CH_3COOH + C_2H_5OH \rightarrow CH_3COOC_2H_5 + H_2O$$

CH_3COOH	C_2H_5OH	$CH_3COOC_2H_5$	H_2O
Ethanoic acid	Ethanol	Ethyl ethanoate	Water

Their names end in '-<u>oate</u>'.
The <u>alcohol</u> forms the <u>first</u> part of the ester's name, and the <u>acid</u> forms the <u>second</u> part.

> ethanol + ethanoic acid → ethyl ethanoate + water
> methanol + propanoic acid → methyl propanoate + water

Esters *Smell Nice but Don't Mix Well with* Water

1) Many esters have <u>pleasant smells</u> — often quite <u>sweet and fruity</u>. They're also <u>volatile</u>. This makes them ideal for perfumes (the evaporated molecules can be detected by smell receptors in your nose).

2) However, many esters are <u>flammable</u> (or even <u>highly</u> flammable). So their volatility also makes them potentially <u>dangerous</u>.

3) Esters <u>don't mix very well with water</u>. (They're not nearly as soluble as alcohols or carboxylic acids.)

4) But esters do mix well with <u>alcohols</u> and other <u>organic solvents</u>.

Esters *are Often Used in* Flavourings *and* Perfumes

1) Because many esters smell nice, they're used in <u>perfumes</u>.

2) Esters are also used to make <u>flavourings</u> and <u>aromas</u> — e.g. there are esters that smell or taste of rum, apple, orange, banana, grape, pineapple, etc.

3) Some esters are used in <u>ointments</u> (they give Deep Heat® its smell).

4) Other esters are used as <u>solvents</u> for paint, ink, glue and in nail varnish remover.

There are things you need to think about when using esters:

1) Inhaling the <u>fumes</u> from some esters <u>irritates mucous membranes</u> in the nose and mouth.

2) <u>Ester fumes</u> are <u>heavier than air</u> and very <u>flammable</u>. Flammable vapour + naked flame = <u>flash fire</u>.

3) Some esters are <u>toxic</u>, especially in large doses. Some people worry about <u>health problems</u> associated with <u>synthetic food additives</u> such as esters.

4) BUT... esters <u>aren't as volatile</u> or as <u>toxic</u> as some other <u>organic solvents</u> — they don't release nearly as many toxic fumes as some of them. In fact esters have <u>replaced solvents</u> such as toluene in many paints and varnishes.

What's a chemist's favourite chocolate — ester eggs...

Who'd have thought those pear drops your gran's such a fan of contained <u>esters</u> instead of pears? It's a crazy old world. Make sure you're clued up on esters before you turn the page.

Revision Summary for Chemistry 3a

Bit of a mixed bag — one minute you're pondering the periodic table, the next you're worrying about how many millions of people are without clean drinking water. The one thing that's constant and unchanging is the need to learn it all for the exam you've got coming up. So test yourself on these little beauties.

1) Before 1800, how were elements classified?
2) Give two reasons why Newlands' Octaves were criticised.
3) Why did Mendeleev leave gaps in his Table of Elements?
4) How are the group number and the number of electrons in the outer shell related?
5) What is shielding?
6) As you go down Group I, what's the trend in reactivity?
7) Describe the density of the alkali metals.
8) Write down the balanced symbol equation for the reaction between sodium and water.
9) Explain why Group 7 elements get less reactive as you go down the group from fluorine to iodine.
10) What is the charge on a halide ion when it forms an ionic compound?
11) Write down the balanced equation for the displacement of bromine from potassium bromide by chlorine.
12) Will the following reactions occur: a) iodine with lithium chloride, b) chlorine with lithium bromide?
13) Describe the physical properties of a typical transition metal.
14) Give an industrial use for transition metals.
15) What are the main ions that cause water hardness?
16) Give two possible health benefits of drinking hard water.
17) Give two methods of removing permanent hardness from water.
18) Describe how you could use titration to compare the hardness of two different water samples.
19) During water treatment, how are microbes killed so that the water is safe to drink?
20) Explain why tap water isn't purified by distillation.
21) Why is fluoride added to some drinking water?
22) What is a reversible reaction? Explain what is meant by an equilibrium.
23) How does changing the temperature and pressure of a reversible reaction alter the equilibrium position?
24) How does this influence the choice of pressure for the Haber process?
25) What determines the choice of operating temperature for the Haber process?
26) What effect does the iron catalyst have on the reaction between nitrogen and hydrogen?
27) Draw the structure of the first three alcohols.
28) When alcohols dissolve in water, is the solution acidic, neutral or alkaline?
29) What gas is formed when alcohols react with sodium?
30) Give two uses of alcohols.
31) What is the functional group in carboxylic acids?
32) Give two uses of carboxylic acids.
33) What two kinds of substance react together to form an ester?
    What catalyst is used in the formation of esters?
34) Write down two uses of esters.

Moles and Titration

There's a nice little experiment you can do to find out how much alkali you need to <u>neutralise</u> an acid. As I'm feeling generous, there's also some useful stuff about <u>moles</u> and <u>concentration</u> thrown in on this page too — you never know when it might come in handy... Probably in the exam though.

"THE MOLE" is Simply the Name Given to a Certain Number

Just like "<u>a million</u>" is this many: 1 000 000; or "<u>a billion</u>" is this many: 1 000 000 000,
"<u>a mole</u>" is this many: 602 300 000 000 000 000 000 000   or 6.023×10^{23}.

1) And that's all it is. <u>Just a number</u>. The burning question, of course, is why is it such a silly long one like that, and with a six at the front?

2) The answer is that when you get <u>precisely that number</u> of atoms of <u>carbon-12</u> it weighs exactly <u>12 g</u>. So, get that number of atoms or molecules, <u>of any element or compound</u>, and conveniently, they <u>weigh</u> exactly the same number of <u>grams</u> as the relative atomic mass, A_r (or M_r) of the element or compound. This is arranged <u>on purpose</u> of course, to make things easier.

3) So, you can use <u>moles</u> as a <u>unit</u> of measurement when you're talking about an amount of a substance.

Concentration is a Measure of How Crowded Things Are

The <u>concentration</u> of a solution can be measured in <u>moles per dm³</u> (i.e. <u>moles per litre</u>).
So 1 mole of stuff in 1 dm³ of solution has a concentration of <u>1 mole per dm³</u> (or 1 mol/dm³).

> The <u>more solute</u> you dissolve in a given volume, the <u>more crowded</u>
> the solute molecules are and the <u>more concentrated</u> the solution.

Concentration can also be measured in <u>grams per dm³</u>. So 56 grams of stuff dissolved in 1 dm³ of solution has a concentration of <u>56 grams per dm³</u>.

| 1 litre |
| = 1000 cm³ |
| = 1 dm³ |

Titrations are Used to Find Out Concentrations

1) You met <u>titrations</u> on page 79. Titrations also allow you to find out <u>exactly</u> how much acid is needed to <u>neutralise</u> a quantity of alkali (or vice versa).

2) You put some <u>alkali</u> in a flask, along with some <u>indicator</u> — <u>phenolphthalein</u> or <u>methyl orange</u>. You don't use universal indicator as it changes colour gradually — and you want a <u>definite</u> colour change.

3) Add the <u>acid</u>, a bit at a time, to the alkali using a <u>burette</u> — giving the flask a regular <u>swirl</u>. Go especially <u>slowly</u> (a drop at a time) when you think the alkali's almost neutralised.

4) The indicator <u>changes colour</u> when <u>all</u> the alkali has been <u>neutralised</u> — phenolphthalein is <u>pink</u> in <u>alkalis</u> but <u>colourless</u> in <u>acids</u>, and methyl orange is <u>yellow</u> in <u>alkalis</u> but <u>red</u> in <u>acids</u>.

5) <u>Record</u> the amount of acid used to <u>neutralise</u> the alkali. It's best to <u>repeat</u> this process a few times, making sure you get (pretty much) the same answer each time.

6) You can then take the <u>mean</u> of your results.

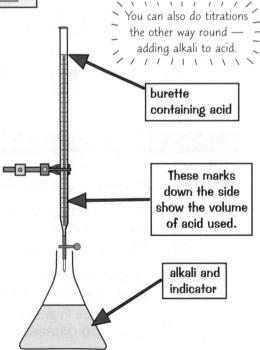

You can also do titrations the other way round — adding alkali to acid.

burette containing acid

These marks down the side show the volume of acid used.

alkali and indicator

If you can spell phenolphthalein, you deserve a GCSE...

There's a little bit at the end of the titration method that's pretty vital when you do <u>any</u> experiment — the bit about <u>repeating</u> the process to check your results. It's all to do with making sure your results are <u>reliable</u>. If you get the same result a number of times, you can have more faith in it than if it's a one-off.

Titration Calculations

I expect you're wondering what you can do with the results from a titration experiment (who wouldn't be). Well, you'll be relieved to know that they can be used to calculate concentrations of acids or alkalis.

You Might Be Asked to Calculate the Concentration

In the exam you might be given the results of a titration experiment and asked to calculate the concentration of the acid when you know the concentration of the alkali (or vice versa).

Example 1: If they ask for concentration in MOLES per dm^3

Say you start off with 25 cm^3 of sodium hydroxide in your flask, and you know that its concentration is 0.1 moles per dm^3.

You then find from your titration that it takes 30 cm^3 of sulfuric acid (whose concentration you don't know) to neutralise the sodium hydroxide.

You can work out the concentration of the acid in moles per dm^3.

> Concentration = moles ÷ volume, so you can make a handy formula triangle.
>
> Concentration (in mol/dm^3) Number of moles
> $$\frac{n}{c \times V}$$
> Volume (in dm^3) One dm^3 is a litre
>
> Cover up the thing you're trying to find — then what's left is the formula you need to use.

Step 1: Work out how many moles of the "known" substance you have using this formula:

Number of moles = concentration × volume
= 0.1 mol/dm^3 × (25 / 1000) dm^3 = 0.0025 moles of NaOH

Remember: 1000 cm^3 = 1 dm^3

Use the formula triangle if it helps.

Step 2: Write down the balanced equation of the reaction...

$$2NaOH + H_2SO_4 \longrightarrow Na_2SO_4 + 2H_2O$$

...and work out how many moles of the "unknown" stuff you must have had.

Using the equation, you can see that for every two moles of sodium hydroxide you had...
...there was just one mole of sulfuric acid.
So if you had 0.0025 moles of sodium hydroxide...
...you must have had 0.0025 ÷ 2 = 0.00125 moles of sulfuric acid.

Step 3: Work out the concentration of the "unknown" stuff.
Concentration = number of moles ÷ volume
= 0.00125 mol ÷ (30 / 1000) dm^3 = 0.041666... mol/dm^3
= 0.0417 mol/dm^3

Don't forget to put the units.

Example 2: If they ask for concentration in GRAMS per dm^3

They might ask you to find out the acid concentration in grams per cubic decimetre (grams per litre). If they do, don't panic — you just need another formula triangle.

Step 1: Work out the relative formula mass for the acid (you should be given the relative atomic masses, e.g. H = 1, S = 32, O = 16):
So, H_2SO_4 = (1 × 2) + 32 + (16 × 4) = 98

Step 2: Convert the concentration in moles (that you've already worked out) into concentration in grams. So, in 1 dm^3:

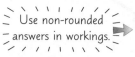
Use non-rounded answers in workings.

Mass in grams = moles × relative formula mass
= 0.041666... × 98 = 4.08333... g
So the concentration in g/dm^3 = 4.08 g/dm^3

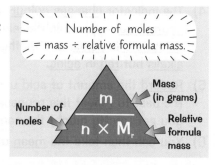
> Number of moles
> = mass ÷ relative formula mass.
>
> Number of moles
> $$\frac{m}{n \times M_r}$$
> Mass (in grams)
> Relative formula mass

Need practice, you do — mmmm...

Scary. But if you get enough practice at these questions, then the fear will evaporate and you can tackle them with a smile on your face and a spring in your step. Remember, don't be baffled by dm^3 — it's just an overly complicated way of saying "litre", that's all. So "moles per dm^3" means "moles per litre". Simple.

Energy

Whenever chemical reactions occur, there are changes in <u>energy</u>. This means that when chemicals get together, things either hot up or cool right off. I'll give you a heads up — this page is a good 'un.

Energy Transfer *can be* Measured

1) You can measure the amount of <u>energy released</u> by a <u>chemical reaction</u> (in solution) by taking the <u>temperature of the reagents</u> (making sure they're the same), <u>mixing</u> them in a <u>polystyrene cup</u> and measuring the <u>temperature of the solution</u> at the <u>end</u> of the reaction. Easy.

2) The biggest <u>problem</u> with energy measurements is the amount of energy <u>lost to the surroundings</u>.

3) You can reduce it a bit by putting the polystyrene cup into a <u>beaker of cotton wool</u> to give <u>more insulation</u>, and putting a <u>lid</u> on the cup to reduce energy lost by <u>evaporation</u>.

4) This method works for reactions of <u>solids with water</u> (e.g. dissolving ammonium nitrate in water) as well as for <u>neutralisation</u> reactions.

> **Example:**
> 1) Place 25 cm³ of dilute hydrochloric acid in a polystyrene cup, and record its temperature.
> 2) Put 25 cm³ of dilute sodium hydroxide in a measuring cylinder and record its temperature.
> 3) As long as they're at the same temperature, add the alkali to the acid and stir.
> 4) Take the temperature of the mixture every 30 seconds, and record the highest temperature it reaches.

This method can also be used where energy is being absorbed — there will be a fall in temperature.

Reactions are Exothermic or Endothermic

> An <u>EXOTHERMIC reaction</u> is one which <u>gives out energy</u> to the surroundings, usually in the form of <u>heat</u> and usually shown by a <u>rise in temperature</u>.

E.g. <u>fuels burning</u> or <u>neutralisation reactions</u>.

> An <u>ENDOTHERMIC reaction</u> is one which <u>takes in energy</u> from the surroundings, usually in the form of <u>heat</u> and usually shown by a <u>fall in temperature</u>.

E.g. <u>photosynthesis</u>.

Energy Must Always be Supplied to Break Bonds...
...and Energy is Always Released When Bonds Form

1) During a chemical reaction, <u>old bonds</u> are <u>broken</u> and <u>new bonds</u> are <u>formed</u>.

2) Energy must be <u>supplied</u> to break <u>existing bonds</u> — so bond breaking is an <u>endothermic</u> process. Energy is <u>released</u> when new bonds are <u>formed</u> — so bond formation is an <u>exothermic</u> process.

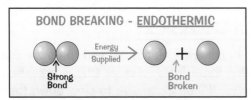

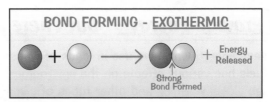

3) In an <u>endothermic</u> reaction, the energy <u>required</u> to break old bonds is <u>greater</u> than the energy <u>released</u> when <u>new bonds</u> are formed.

4) In an <u>exothermic</u> reaction, the energy <u>released</u> in bond formation is <u>greater</u> than the energy used in <u>breaking</u> old bonds.

Save energy — break fewer bonds...

You can get <u>cooling packs</u> that use an <u>endothermic</u> reaction to draw heat from an injury. The pack contains two compartments with different chemicals in. When you use it, you snap the partition and the chemicals <u>mix</u> and <u>react</u>, taking in <u>heat</u> — pretty cool, I reckon (no pun intended).

Energy and Fuels

Burning <u>fuels</u> releases <u>energy</u>. Just how much energy you can find using <u>calorimetry</u>. Bet you can't wait.

Fuel Energy is Calculated Using Calorimetry

Different fuels produce <u>different amounts of energy</u>. To measure the amount of energy released when a fuel is burnt, you can simply burn the fuel and use the flame to <u>heat up some water</u>. Of course, this has to have a fancy chemistry name — <u>calorimetry</u>. Calorimetry uses a <u>glass</u> or <u>metal container</u> (it's usually made of <u>copper</u> because copper conducts heat so well).

Method:

1) Put 50 g of water in the copper can and <u>record its temperature</u>.

2) <u>Weigh the spirit burner</u> and lid.

3) Put the spirit burner underneath the can, and light the wick. Heat the water, <u>stirring constantly</u>, until the temperature reaches about <u>50 °C</u>.

4) <u>Put out the flame</u> using the burner lid, and measure the <u>final temperature</u> of the water.

5) <u>Weigh</u> the spirit burner and lid <u>again</u>.

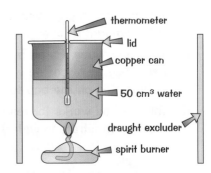

- thermometer
- lid
- copper can
- 50 cm³ water
- draught excluder
- spirit burner

Example: to work out the energy per gram of methylated spirit (meths):

1) Mass of spirit burner + lid before heating = **68.75 g**

2) Mass of spirit burner + lid after heating = **67.85 g**

→ Mass of meths burnt = 0.9 g

3) Temperature of water in copper can before heating = **21.5 °C**

4) Temperature of water in copper can after heating = **52.5 °C**

→ Temperature change in 50 g of water due to heating = 31.0 °C

5) So 0.9 g of fuel produces enough energy to heat up 50 g of water by 31 °C.

6) It takes 4.2 joules of energy to heat up 1 g of water by 1 °C. *You'll be told this in the exam.* This is known as the specific heat capacity of water.

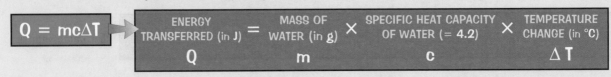

$$Q = mc\Delta T$$

| ENERGY TRANSFERRED (in J) | = | MASS OF WATER (in g) | × | SPECIFIC HEAT CAPACITY OF WATER (= 4.2) | × | TEMPERATURE CHANGE (in °C) |
| Q | | m | | c | | ΔT |

7) Therefore, the energy produced in this experiment = 50 × 4.2 × 31 = <u>6510 joules</u>.

8) So 0.9 g of meths produces 6510 joules of energy...

... meaning 1 g of meths produces 6510/0.9 = <u>7233 J or 7.233 kJ</u>

Energy's wasted heating the can, air, etc. — so this figure will often be much lower than the actual energy content.

You can use pretty much the same method to calculate the amount of energy produced by <u>foods</u>. The only problem is that when you set food on fire, it tends to <u>go out</u> after a bit.

Fuels Provide Energy — But There are Consequences

Fuels release <u>energy</u> which we use in loads of ways — e.g. to generate electricity and to power cars. Burning fuels has various effects on the <u>environment</u>. Burning fossil fuels releases CO_2, a greenhouse gas. This causes <u>global warming</u> and other types of <u>climate change</u>. It'll be <u>expensive</u> to slow down these effects, and to put things right. Developing alternative energy sources (e.g. tidal power) costs money.

Crude oil is <u>running out</u>. We use <u>a lot of fuels</u> made from crude oil (e.g. <u>petrol and diesel</u>) and as it runs out it will get more expensive. This means that everything that's <u>transported</u> by lorry, train or plane gets more expensive too. So the <u>price of crude oil</u> has a big economic effect.

Energy from fuels — it's a burning issue...

Alrighty. A bit of <u>method</u>, a few <u>sums</u> and some <u>social 'n' environmental gubbins</u> to round it off. A useful thing to remember is that energy values can be measured in <u>calories</u> instead of joules (1 calorie = 4.2 joules). More importantly though, make sure you're familiar with the equation $Q = mc\Delta T$ — you're bound to need it.

Bond Energies

This is about <u>calculating</u> the stuff that you found by experiment on the previous page.

Energy Level Diagrams _Show if it's_ Exo- _or_ Endo-thermic

In exothermic reactions ΔH is –ve ← ΔH is the energy change.

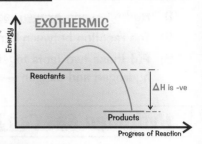

1) This shows an <u>exothermic reaction</u> — the products are at a <u>lower energy</u> than the reactants. The difference in <u>height</u> represents the energy <u>given out</u> in the reaction (per mole). ΔH is –ve here.

2) The <u>initial rise</u> in the line represents the energy needed to <u>break</u> the old bonds. This is the <u>activation energy</u>.

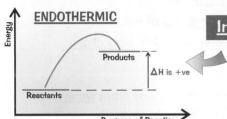

In endothermic reactions ΔH is +ve

1) This shows an <u>endothermic reaction</u> because the products are at a <u>higher energy</u> than the reactants, so ΔH <u>is +ve</u>.

2) The <u>difference in height</u> represents the <u>energy taken in</u> during the reaction (per mole).

The <u>Activation Energy</u> is <u>Lowered</u> by <u>Catalysts</u>

1) The <u>activation energy</u> represents the <u>minimum energy</u> needed by reacting particles to <u>break their bonds</u>.

2) A <u>catalyst</u> provides a <u>different pathway</u> for a reaction that has a <u>lower activation energy</u> (so the reaction happens more easily and more quickly).

3) This is represented by the <u>lower curve</u> on the diagram showing a <u>lower activation energy</u>.

4) The <u>overall energy change</u> for the reaction, ΔH, <u>remains the same</u> though.

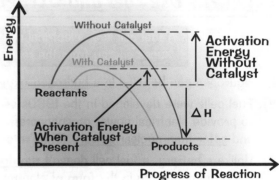

Bond Energy Calculations — _Need to be Practised_

1) <u>Every</u> chemical bond has a particular <u>bond energy</u> associated with it. This <u>bond energy</u> varies slightly depending on what <u>compound</u> the bond occurs in. Don't worry — you'll be given the ones you need.

2) You can use these <u>known bond energies</u> to calculate the <u>overall energy change</u> for a reaction. You need to <u>practise</u> a few of these, but the basic idea is really very simple...

Example: _The Formation of HCl_

Using known bond energies you can <u>calculate</u> the <u>energy change</u> for this reaction:

$$H — H + Cl — Cl \rightarrow 2H — Cl$$
$$H_2 + Cl_2 \rightarrow 2HCl$$

The bond energies you need are: H—H: +436 kJ/mol; Cl—Cl: +242 kJ/mol; H—Cl: +431 kJ/mol.

1) <u>Breaking</u> one mole of H—H and one mole of Cl—Cl bonds <u>requires</u> 436 + 242 = <u>678 kJ</u>

2) <u>Forming</u> <u>two</u> moles of H—Cl bonds <u>releases</u> 2 × 431 = <u>862 kJ</u>

3) <u>Overall</u> more energy is <u>released</u> than is used to form the products: 862 – 678 = <u>184 kJ/mol</u> released.

4) Since this is energy <u>released</u>, if we wanted to show ΔH we'd need to put a <u>negative sign</u> in front of it to indicate that it's an <u>exothermic</u> reaction, like this: ΔH = –184 kJ/mol

Energy transfer — make sure you take it all in...

I admit — it's a bit like maths, this. But think how many times you've heard <u>energy efficiency</u> mentioned — well, this kind of calculation is used in working out whether we're using resources efficiently or not.

Getting Energy from Hydrogen

There are two ways you can use hydrogen as a fuel — by burning it in an engine or by using it in a fuel cell...

Hydrogen and Oxygen Give Out Energy When They React

1) Hydrogen and oxygen react to produce water — which isn't a pollutant.
2) The reaction between hydrogen and oxygen is exothermic — it releases energy.
3) Put these two facts together, and you get something useful: you can get energy by reacting hydrogen and oxygen — either in a combustion engine or in a fuel cell.

Hydrogen Gas Can be Burnt to Power Vehicles

1) Hydrogen gas can be burnt in oxygen as a fuel in the combustion engines of vehicles.
2) Pros: Hydrogen combines with oxygen in the air to form just water — so it's very clean.

hydrogen + oxygen → water

3) Cons: You need a special, expensive engine. Although hydrogen can be made from water, which there's plenty of, you still need to use energy from another source to make it. Also, hydrogen's hard to store safely — it's very explosive.

Fuel Cells Use Fuel and Oxygen to Produce Electrical Energy

> A fuel cell is an electrical cell that's supplied with a fuel and oxygen and uses energy from the reaction between them to generate electricity.

1) Hydrogen can be used in a hydrogen-oxygen fuel cell.
2) Fuel cells were developed in the 1960s as part of the space programme, to provide electrical power on spacecraft — they were more practical than solar cells and safer than nuclear power. (They're still used on the Space Shuttle missions.)
3) Unlike a battery, a fuel cell doesn't run down or need recharging from the mains. It'll produce energy in the form of electricity and heat as long as fuel is supplied.

The Car Industry is Developing Fuel Cells

1) The car industry is developing fuel cells to replace conventional petrol/diesel engines.
2) Fuel cell vehicles don't produce any conventional pollutants — no greenhouse gases, no nitrogen oxides, no sulfur dioxide, no carbon monoxide. The only by-products are water and heat. This would be a major advantage in cities, where air pollution from traffic is a big problem.
3) Fuel cells could eventually help countries to become less dependent on crude oil.
4) However, they're not likely to mean the end of either conventional power stations or our dependence on fossil fuels. That's because:

   - hydrogen is a gas so it takes up loads more space to store than liquid fuels like petrol.
   - it's very explosive so it's difficult to store safely.
   - the hydrogen fuel is often made either from hydrocarbons (from fossil fuels), or by electrolysis of water, which uses electricity (and that electricity's got to be generated somehow — usually this involves fossil fuels).

Fuel cells — they're simply electrifying...

Using hydrogen as a fuel sounds great — but you have to think. Once you've got the hydrogen, yeah, it's ace. But producing that hydrogen takes a lot of energy, which might not be from renewable sources. That doesn't mean energy from hydrogen won't be important in the future, only that you need to look at the whole picture.

Tests for Positive Ions

Forensic science involves a lot of chemical tests, which is what these next two pages are about. Before you start reading, you have to pretend you have a mystery substance. You don't know what it is, but you need to find out — just like that bloke off the telly who investigates murders.

If it's an ionic compound it'll have a positive and a negative part. So, first off, some tests for positive ions.

Flame Tests **Identify** Metal Ions

Remember, metals always form positive ions.

Compounds of some metals burn with a characteristic colour, as you see every November 5th when a firework explodes. So, remember, remember...

1) You can test for various metal ions by putting your substance in a flame and seeing what colour the flame goes.

> Lithium, Li^+, gives a crimson flame.
> Sodium, Na^+, gives a yellow flame.
> Potassium, K^+, gives a lilac flame.
> Calcium, Ca^{2+}, gives a red flame.
> Barium, Ba^{2+}, gives a green flame.

2) To flame-test a compound in the lab, dip a clean wire loop into a sample of the compound, and put the wire loop in the clear blue part of the Bunsen flame (the hottest bit). First make sure the wire loop is really clean by dipping it into hydrochloric acid and rinsing it with distilled water.

Some Metal Ions **Form a** Coloured Precipitate **with** NaOH

This is also a test for metal ions, but it's slightly more involved. Concentrate now...

1) Many metal hydroxides are insoluble and precipitate out of solution when formed. Some of these hydroxides have a characteristic colour.

2) So in this test you add a few drops of sodium hydroxide solution to a solution of your mystery compound — all in the hope of forming an insoluble hydroxide.

3) If you get a coloured insoluble hydroxide you can then tell which metal was in the compound.

"Metal"	Colour of precipitate	Ionic Reaction
Calcium, Ca^{2+}	White	$Ca^{2+}_{(aq)} + 2OH^-_{(aq)} \rightarrow Ca(OH)_{2\,(s)}$
Copper(II), Cu^{2+}	Blue	$Cu^{2+}_{(aq)} + 2OH^-_{(aq)} \rightarrow Cu(OH)_{2\,(s)}$
Iron(II), Fe^{2+}	Green	$Fe^{2+}_{(aq)} + 2OH^-_{(aq)} \rightarrow Fe(OH)_{2\,(s)}$
Iron(III), Fe^{3+}	Brown	$Fe^{3+}_{(aq)} + 3OH^-_{(aq)} \rightarrow Fe(OH)_{3\,(s)}$
Aluminium, Al^{3+}	White at first. But then redissolves in excess NaOH to form a colourless solution.	$Al^{3+}_{(aq)} + 3OH^-_{(aq)} \rightarrow Al(OH)_{3\,(s)}$ then $Al(OH)_{3\,(s)} + OH^-_{(aq)} \rightarrow Al(OH)^-_{4\,(aq)}$
Magnesium, Mg^{2+}	White	$Mg^{2+}_{(aq)} + 2OH^-_{(aq)} \rightarrow Mg(OH)_{2\,(s)}$

Testing metals is flaming useful...

Remember... your metal ion is your positive ion. To find out what your mystery ion is, start off with a flame test. If that doesn't give you any exciting colours, then go on and try the sodium hydroxide test. But don't forget that you can use a flame test or a precipitate test to identify calcium ions, although sadly you're looking for a different colour in each type of test. Looks like there's no easy way around it. I'd learn all the colours on this page and the metal ions they match up to — you might need any one of them in the exam.

Tests for Negative Ions

So now maybe you know what the <u>positive</u> part of your mystery substance is (see previous page).
Now it's time to test for the <u>negative</u> bit.

Testing for Carbonates — Check for CO_2

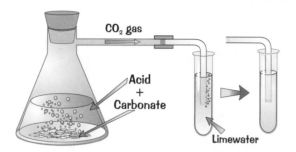

CO$_2$ gas

Acid + Carbonate

Limewater

First things first — the test for carbon dioxide (CO_2).

1) You can test to see if a gas is <u>carbon dioxide</u> by bubbling it through <u>limewater</u>. If it is <u>carbon dioxide</u>, the <u>limewater turns cloudy</u>.

2) You can use this to test for <u>carbonate</u> ions (CO_3^{2-}), since carbonates react with <u>dilute acids</u> to form <u>carbon dioxide</u>.

Acid + Carbonate → Salt + Water + Carbon dioxide

Tests for Halides and Sulfates

You can test for certain ions by seeing if a <u>precipitate</u> is formed after these reactions...

Halide Ions

To test for <u>chloride</u> (Cl⁻), <u>bromide</u> (Br⁻) or <u>iodide</u> (I⁻) ions, add <u>dilute nitric acid</u> (HNO_3), followed by <u>silver nitrate solution</u> ($AgNO_3$).

A <u>chloride</u> gives a white precipitate of <u>silver chloride</u>.

$$Ag^+_{(aq)} + Cl^-_{(aq)} \longrightarrow AgCl_{(s)}$$

A <u>bromide</u> gives a cream precipitate of <u>silver bromide</u>.

$$Ag^+_{(aq)} + Br^-_{(aq)} \longrightarrow AgBr_{(s)}$$

An <u>iodide</u> gives a yellow precipitate of <u>silver iodide</u>.

$$Ag^+_{(aq)} + I^-_{(aq)} \longrightarrow AgI_{(s)}$$

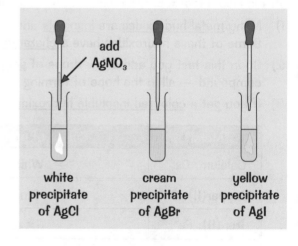

add AgNO$_3$

white precipitate of AgCl

cream precipitate of AgBr

yellow precipitate of AgI

Sulfate Ions

1) To test for a <u>sulfate</u> ion (SO_4^{2-}), <u>add dilute HCl</u>, followed by <u>barium chloride solution</u>, $BaCl_2$.

2) A <u>white</u> precipitate of <u>barium sulfate</u> means the original compound was a sulfate.

$$Ba^{2+}_{(aq)} + SO_4^{2-}_{(aq)} \longrightarrow BaSO_{4(s)}$$

Sherlock never looked so good in a lab coat...

So you might have to do loads of different chemical tests to find out all the information about your mystery substance. It's a bit like detective work — eliminating suspects, narrowing down possibilities, and so on. It's the kind of stuff <u>exam questions</u> are made of, by the way, so be warned. They might give you the <u>results</u> from several chemical tests, and you have to say what the substance is.

Revision Summary for Chemistry 3b

Whenever anything at all happens, energy is either taken in or released. So it's amazingly important. If that doesn't inspire you to learn the stuff about it, the fact that you're likely to get exam questions on it should. There's also titration and bagloads of chemical tests in this section too. There's no easy way to remember it all — you just have to do some good old-fashioned memorising. Anyway, enough words of wisdom, try these questions:

1) Name a suitable indicator you could use in the titration of sulfuric acid and sodium hydroxide.

2)* In a titration, 49 cm³ of hydrochloric acid was required to neutralise 25 cm³ of sodium hydroxide with a concentration of 0.2 moles per dm³.
   Calculate the concentration of the hydrochloric acid in: a) mol/dm³   b) g/dm³

3) An acid and an alkali were mixed in a polystyrene cup, as shown to the right.
   The acid and alkali were each at 20 °C before they were mixed.
   After they were mixed, the temperature of the solution reached 24 °C.
   a) State whether this reaction is exothermic or endothermic.
   b) Explain why the cotton wool is used.

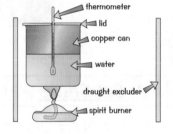
20 cm³ of dilute sulfuric acid + 20 cm³ of dilute sodium hydroxide solution
cotton wool

4) Is energy released when bonds are formed or when bonds are broken?

5) The apparatus below is used to measure how much energy is released when pentane is burnt. It takes 4.2 joules of energy to heat 1 g of water by 1 °C.

   a)*Using the following data, and the equation $Q = mc \, \Delta T$,
      calculate the amount of energy per gram of pentane.

Mass of empty copper can	64 g	Initial temperature of water	17 °C
Mass of copper can + water	116 g	Final temperature of water	47 °C

Mass of spirit burner + pentane before burning	97.72 g
Mass of spirit burner + pentane after burning	97.37 g

thermometer
lid
copper can
water
draught excluder
spirit burner

   b) A data book says that pentane has 49 kJ/g of energy. Why is the amount you calculated different?

6) Explain why the price of bananas might rise if we keep burning so much fuel.

7) a) Draw energy level diagrams for exothermic and endothermic reactions.
   b) Explain how bond breaking and forming relate to these diagrams.

8) What is the activation energy for a reaction? Mark it on your exothermic energy level diagram from Q7.

9) How does a catalyst affect: a) activation energy,   b) overall energy change for a reaction?

10)*a) Calculate the energy change for the following reaction:
       $$2H_2 + O_2 \rightarrow 2H_2O \qquad 2H-H + O-O \rightarrow 2H-O-H$$
    You need these bond energies: H–H: +436 kJ/mol, O=O: +496 kJ/mol, O–H: +463 kJ/mol

    b) Is this an exothermic or endothermic reaction?

11) Give an advantage of using hydrogen as a fuel in a car engine.

12) Give a disadvantage of using hydrogen as a fuel in a car engine.

13) What is a fuel cell?

14) Why is the car industry researching fuel cells?

15) Describe two ways of testing for metal ions.

16) How would you distinguish between solutions of: a) magnesium sulfate and aluminium sulfate,
    b) sodium bromide and sodium iodide,   c) copper nitrate and copper sulfate?

* Answers on page 100.

The Perfect Cup of Tea

The making and drinking of tea are important life skills. It's not something that will crop up in the exam, but it is something that will make your revision much easier. So here's a guide to making the perfect cuppa...

1) Choose the Right Mug

A good mug is an essential part of the tea drinking experience, but choosing the right vessel for your tea can be tricky. Here's a guide to choosing your mug:

Some bad mugs:

No handles.

Too fancy (and saucers are for grannies).

Too flimsy and too 80s.

Too many handles.

The perfect mug:

Holds just the right amount of tea.

Wide enough to dunk a biscuit.

Has a design that complements your personality (yes, I'm a bit hippy).

Nice, easy to hold handle.

2) Get Some Water and Boil It

For a really great brew follow these easy step-by-step instructions:

1) First, pour some water into a kettle and switch it on. (Check it's switched on at the wall too.)

2) Let the kettle boil. While you're waiting, see what's on TV later and check your belly button for fluff. Oh, and put a tea bag in a mug.

3) Once the kettle has boiled, pour the water into the mug.

4) Mash the tea bag about a bit with a spoon. Remove the tea bag.

5) Add a splash of milk (and a lump of sugar or two if you're feeling naughty).

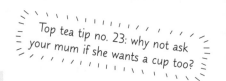

Top tea tip no. 23: why not ask your mum if she wants a cup too?

Note: some people may tell you to add the milk before the tea. Scientists have recently confirmed that this is nonsense.

3) Sit Back and Relax

Now this is important — once you've made your cuppa:

1) Have a quick rummage in the kitchen cupboards for a cheeky biscuit. (Custard creams are best — steer clear of any ginger biscuits — they're evil.)

2) Find your favourite armchair/beanbag. Move the cat.

3) Sit back and enjoy your mug of tea. You've earned it.

Phew — time for a brew I reckon...

It's best to ignore what other people say about making cups of tea and follow this method. Trust me, this is the most definitive and effective method. If you don't do it this way, you'll have a shoddy drinking experience. There, you've been warned. Now go and get the kettle on. Mine's milk and two sugars...

Index

Index

Index

Answers

<u>Revision Summary for Chemistry 1a (page 30)</u>

3) Calcium

7) a)

Could be hydrogen/oxygen/nitrogen (or any other diatomic gaseous element).

b)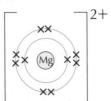

Could be carbon dioxide (water molecules are bent).

8) a) $CaCO_3 + 2HCl \rightarrow CaCl_2 + H_2O + CO_2$

b) $Ca + 2H_2O \rightarrow Ca(OH)_2 + H_2$

29) Propane — the fuel needs to be a gas at –10 °C to work in a camping stove.

<u>Revision Summary for Chemistry 1b (page 41)</u>

22) b) 2 cm   c) 3.5 years

<u>Example on page 49</u>

A is simple molecular, B is giant metallic, C is giant covalent, D is giant ionic

<u>Bottom of page 52</u>

1) Cu: 63.5, K: 39, Kr: 84, Cl: 35.5

2) NaOH: 40, Fe_2O_3: 160, C_6H_{14}: 86, $Mg(NO_3)_2$: 148

<u>Bottom of page 53</u>

1) a) 30.0% b) 88.9% c) 48.0%
   d) 65.3%

2) CH_4

<u>Bottom of page 54</u>

1) 21.4 g

2) 38.0 g

<u>Revision Summary for Chemistry 2a (page 57)</u>

9) a) KCl   b) $CaCl_2$

10)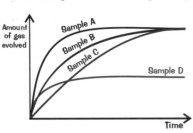

16) A: giant metallic, B: giant covalent, C: giant ionic

21) a) 40 b) 108 c) 44 d) 84 e) 106 f) 81
    g) 56 h) 17

23) a)i) 12.0% ii) 27.3% iii) 75.0%
    b)i) 74.2% ii) 70.0% iii) 52.9%

24) $MgSO_4$

25) 80.3 g

<u>Revision Summary for Chemistry 2b (page 72)</u>

3) b)

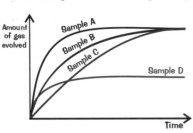

<u>Revision Summary for Chemistry 3b (page 95)</u>

2) a) No. of moles NaOH = $0.2 \times (25 \div 1000)$
      = 0.005
      $HCl + NaOH \rightarrow NaCl + H_2O$, so no. of moles HCl = 0.005
      Concentration HCl (moles per dm^3)
      = $0.005 \div (49 \div 1000)$
      = <u>0.102 moles per dm^3</u>

   b) M_r HCl = $1 + 35.5 = 36.5$
      mass = number of moles $\times M_r$
      = $0.102 \times 36.5 =$ <u>3.72 grams per dm^3</u>

5) a) Mass of water heated = $116\ g - 64\ g = 52\ g$
      Temperature rise of water = $47\ °C - 17\ °C = 30\ °C$
      Mass of pentane burnt = $97.72\ g - 97.37\ g$ = 0.35 g

      So 0.35 g of pentane provides enough energy to heat up 52 g of water by 30 °C.

      It takes 4.2 joules of energy to heat up 1 g of water by 1 °C.

      $Q = mc\ \Delta T$. Therefore, the energy produced in this experiment is $52 \times 4.2 \times 30 = 6552$ J.

      So, 0.35 g of pentane produces 6552 J of energy... meaning 1 g of pentane produces 6552/0.35 = <u>18 720 J or 18.720 kJ</u>

10) a) Bonds broken: 2 moles of H–H bonds
       = $2 \times 436 = 872$ kJ
       1 mole of O=O bonds = 496 kJ
       Total energy needed to break bonds
       = $872 + 496 = 1368$ kJ

       Bonds made: 2 moles of (2 × O–H bonds)
       = $2 \times 2 \times 463 = 1852$ kJ
       Overall more energy is released than is used, so $1852 - 1368 =$ <u>484 kJ/mol is released.</u>

    b) This is an exothermic reaction.